# Programming Made Simple

**C Programming**
EXTON
750632445    1997

**C++ Programming**
EXTON
750632437    1997

**COBOL**
EXTON
750638346    1998

**Delphi Version 5**    NEW!
MORRIS
750651881    2000

**Delphi**
MORRIS
750632461    1997

**HTML 4.0**
MCBRIDE
750641789    1999

**Java**
MCBRIDE, P K
750632410    1997

**Javascript**
MCBRIDE, P K
750637978    1997

**Pascal**
MCBRIDE, P K
750632429    1997

**Visual Basic**
MORRIS
0750632453    1997

**Visual C++**
MORRIS
0750635703    1998

## UPCOMING in 2001

**Visual Basic Version 6**
MORRIS
075065189X

ALL
YOU NEED
TO GET
STARTED!

MADE SIMPLE
BOOKS

# Computing Made Simple

**Access 2000**
STEPHEN
0750641827     1999

**Access 2000 Business Edition**
STEPHEN
075064611X     1999

**Access 97 for Windows**
STEPHEN
0750638001     1997

**CompuServe 2000**     NEW!
BRINDLEY
0750645245     2000

**Designing Internet Home Pages
2nd edition**
HOBBS
0750644761     1999

**ECDL/ICDL Version 3.0**     NEW!
BCD
0750651873     2000

**Excel 2000**
MORRIS
0750641800     2000

**Excel 2000 Business Edition**
MORRIS
0750646098     2000

**Excel 97 for Windows**
MORRIS
0750638028     1997

**Excel for Windows 95 (V. 7)**
MORRIS
0750628162     1996

**Explorer 5**
MCBRIDE, P K
0750646276     1999

**Frontpage 2000**
MCBRIDE, Nat
0750645989     1999

**FrontPage 97**
MCBRIDE, Nat
0750639415     1998

**iMac and iBook**     NEW!
BRINDLEY
075064608X     2000

**Internet In Colour
2nd edition**
MCBRIDE, P K
0750645768     1999

**Internet for Windows 98**
MCBRIDE, P K
0750645636     1999

**MS DOS**
SINCLAIR
0750620692     1994

**Office 2000**
MCBRIDE, P K
0750641797     1999

**Office 97**
MCBRIDE, P K
0750637986     1997

**Outlook 2000**     NEW!
MCBRIDE, P K
0750644141     2000

**Photoshop**
WYNNE-POWELL
075064334X     1999

**Pocket PC**     NEW!
PEACOCK
0750649003     2000

**Powerpoint 2000**
STEPHEN
0750641770     1999

**Powerpoint 97 for Windows**
STEPHEN
0750637994     1997

**Publisher 2000**
STEPHEN
0750645970     1999

**Publisher 97**
STEPHEN
0750639431     1998

**Sage Accounts**
McBRIDE
0750644133     1999

**Searching the Internet**
MCBRIDE, P K
0750637943     1998

**Windows 98**
MCBRIDE, P K
0750640391     1998

**Windows 95**
MCBRIDE, P K
0750623063     1995

**Windows CE**
PEACOCK
0750643358     1999

**Windows ME**     NEW!
MCBRIDE, P K
0750652373     2000

**Windows NT**
HOBBS
0750635118     1997

**Word 2000**
BRINDLEY
0750641819     1999

**Word 2000 Business Edition**
BRINDLEY
0750646101     2000

**Word 97 for Windows**
BRINDLEY
075063801X     1997

**Word 7 for Windows 95**
BRINDLEY
0750628154     1996

**Works 2000**
MCBRIDE, P K
0750649852     2000

## UPCOMING in 2001

**Basic Computer Skills**
SHERMAN
075064897X

**ECDL/ICDL 3.0
Office 2000 Edition**
BCD
0750653388

**Microsoft Project 2000**
MURPHY
0750651903

**ALL
YOU NEED
TO GET
STARTED!**

MADE SIMPLE
BOOKS

# HTML 4.0
# Made Simple

P.K. McBride

Nat McBride

**MADE SIMPLE**
**BOOKS**

OXFORD AUCKLAND BOSTON JOHANNESBURG MELBOURNE NEW DELHI

Made Simple
An imprint of Butterworth-Heinemann
Linacre House, Jordan Hill, Oxford OX2 8DP
A division of Reed Educational and Professional Publishing Ltd

R    A member of the Reed Elsevier plc group

First published 1999
Reprinted 1999, 2000, 2001

TRADEMARKS/REGISTERED TRADEMARKS
Computer hardware and software brand names mentioned in this book are protected
by their respective trademarks and are acknowledged.

**British Library Cataloguing in Publication Data**
A catalogue record for this book is available from the British Library

ISBN 0 7506 4178 9

Typeset by P.K.McBride, Southampton

Archtype and Bash Casual fonts from Advanced Graphics Ltd
Icons designed by Sarah Ward © 1994
Printed and bound in Great Britain by Scotprint

FOR EVERY TITLE THAT WE PUBLISH, BUTTERWORTH-HEINEMANN
WILL PAY FOR BTCV TO PLANT AND CARE FOR A TREE.

# Contents

Preface ................................................................. IX

| | | |
|---|---|---|
| 1 | **Introducing HTML** | **1** |

What is HTML? ........................................................ 2
HTML documents ...................................................... 4
Key concepts ........................................................ 6
Writing HTML ........................................................ 8
HTML editors ....................................................... 10
Editors and hand-coding ............................................ 13
Useful software .................................................... 14
Summary ............................................................ 18

| | | |
|---|---|---|
| 2 | **Working with text** | **19** |

Plain text and headings ............................................ 20
Alignment .......................................................... 23
Text appearance .................................................... 25
Size ............................................................... 28
Colour ............................................................. 29
Typefaces .......................................................... 32
Lists .............................................................. 34
Summary ............................................................ 36

| | | |
|---|---|---|
| 3 | **Links** | **37** |

Hypertext .......................................................... 38
Links within a page ................................................ 40
Multi-page structures .............................................. 42
Mailto: me ......................................................... 46
Other links ........................................................ 47
Summary ............................................................ 48

## 4     Graphics     49

Using graphics on your site ............................................ 50
Creating images ............................................................ 52
GIFs .............................................................................. 55
JPEGs ........................................................................... 57
Background images ...................................................... 58
Positioning and alignment ........................................... 60
Size .............................................................................. 62
Borders and spacing .................................................... 64
Links ............................................................................. 65
Image maps .................................................................. 66
Summary ...................................................................... 70

## 5     Page layout     71

Layout methods ............................................................ 72
Simple tables ............................................................... 74
Formatting tables ......................................................... 76
Cell size ....................................................................... 80
Advanced tables ........................................................... 82
Borders and rules ......................................................... 86
Tables for page layout ................................................. 88
Frames .......................................................................... 92
Filling in the frames .................................................... 94
Links and targets ......................................................... 95
Changing a frame's look .............................................. 97
Summary ...................................................................... 98

## 6     Cascading Style Sheets     99

Style sheets ................................................................ 100
Elements and inheritance ........................................... 102

Font attributes ............................................................ 104

Text attributes ........................................................... 106

Colours and backgrounds ........................................ 108

Margins and borders ................................................. 110

Classes and IDs ......................................................... 112

Contained styles ........................................................ 114

Structured sheets ...................................................... 115

Positioning elements ................................................ 117

External style sheets ................................................. 120

Summary ...................................................................... 122

## 7    Forms      123

Gathering feedback ................................................... 124

Text inputs .................................................................. 126

Checkboxes and radio buttons .............................. 128

Drop-down menus .................................................... 130

Buttons ......................................................................... 132

Custom buttons ......................................................... 133

Refining your form ................................................... 134

Forms for Javascript ................................................. 137

Summary ...................................................................... 138

## 8    Sound and animation      139

Putting sound on the page ...................................... 140

Recording sound ....................................................... 142

RealAudio .................................................................... 144

Video clips ................................................................... 145

Animations .................................................................. 146

Flash and Shockwave ............................................... 148

Marquees ..................................................................... 149

Summary ...................................................................... 150

## 9  Active pages                                   151

Programming languages ........................................................... 152
JavaScript ................................................................................... 153
Working with objects ............................................................... 155
The Status line ......................................................................... 157
Feedback on-line ..................................................................... 159
CGI ............................................................................................... 162
Java applets ............................................................................. 164
Summary ................................................................................... 168

## 10  Publishing your pages                         169

Organising your files ............................................................... 170
Keywords ................................................................................... 172
Uploading with WS_FTP ......................................................... 174
Publishing wizards ................................................................... 176
Summary ................................................................................... 178

## Reference section                                 179

Tags and options ..................................................................... 180
Character codes ....................................................................... 188
Style sheets ............................................................................. 189
Links ........................................................................................... 193

## Index                                             195

# Preface

This is a practical text for people who want to create their own Web pages. It assumes that you know little or nothing about HTML, but that you want to learn it quickly, thoroughly and without getting bogged down in theory. All it assumes is that you have a computer and a browser, and that you are reasonably familar with both.

The essentials of HTML are easy to master – you can learn enough to knock up a small, but well-formed Web site over a weekend. It will take you a little longer to work right through this book, but we hope that you will find it worth the trouble. We have tried to give as full a coverage of HTML as is possible within its 200 pages, though we know we have skated over a few of the more obscure features and of those browser-specific extensions that Microsoft and Netscape have introduced during the course of the 'browser wars'.

All you need for simple text-and-images pages is covered in the first four chapters. The next two describe a range of techniques for positioning and formatting material. Tables and frames (Chapter 5) can be handled by almost all browsers nowadays, but if you choose to use style sheets (Chapter 6) you have to accept that only people with newer browsers will see your pages in all their glory. If you want feedback from your visitors – orders for your products, input from your club's members, or simply comments on your site – you need forms (Chapter 7). They can be fiddly to set up, but are worth it. In Chapter 8 we look at adding sounds and animations to liven up your pages, then dip into the Web programming languages to see how they can produce more active and interactive sites.

You don't have to wait until you've read right to the end before publishing your pages. Jump to Chapter 10 when you've created enough to make a good site. You can always upload new or improved pages later – and you should do so regularly if you want to keep your visitors coming back for more.

The document and image files for the larger examples can be found on the Programming Web pages at the Made Simple site, at:

> http://www.madesimple.co.uk

HTML is there to be used creatively. We've had fun writing this book and we hope that you have as much fun using it.

*Mac and Nat, January 1999*

# Update notes

We've taken the opportunity of this reprint to do a little updating. HTML 4.0 hasn't changed since we wrote this book two years ago, but new versions of the browsers have appeared. While these aren't dramatically different from the earlier versions, there are a couple of significant changes.

Previously there had been a few features of HTML that were not handled – or not handled properly – by Netscape. That has been fixed. Netscape 6.0 interprets HTML in almost exactly the same way as Internet Explorer (in versions 4.0 and higher).If you are using one of these newer browsers, you need to be aware that some features are not implemented by earlier software. Look out for the 'new browsers' references.

The new Windows Media Player can handle streaming audio and video – which previously only Real players had been able to cope with. New material has been added to cover this.

*Mac and Nat, March 2001*

# 1 Introducing HTML

What is HTML? . . . . . . . . . . . . . . . . . 2

HTML documents . . . . . . . . . . . . . . . 4

Key concepts . . . . . . . . . . . . . . . . . 6

Writing HTML . . . . . . . . . . . . . . . . 8

HTML editors . . . . . . . . . . . . . . . . .10

Editors and hand-coding . . . . . . . . . .13

Useful software . . . . . . . . . . . . . . .14

Summary . . . . . . . . . . . . . . . . . . .18

# What is HTML?

HTML – HyperText Markup Language – is the system that underpins the World Wide Web. It tells browsers how to display text and graphics, and creates the links between Web pages.

HTML is a simpler, specialised sub-set of SGML – Standard Generalized Markup Language – a platform-independent document formatting system. This is highly flexible, very complicated and irrelevant to most HTML users. If you want to know more about SGML, there's lots of documentation on it on the Internet – look for 'SGML' at any search engine – but there's no space to discuss it here.

The history of HTML is very interesting – and you can look up the details on the Internet if you are into that sort of thing. For practical purposes, you just need to know a few crucial things about its development.

## The background

HTML and browsers have developed in tandem, driven forwards largely by rivalry between the browser manufacturers – principally Microsoft and Netscape Corporation. Most – though not all – of the new features developed by one or other, to make their browser better, have been accepted by the rival and incorporated into the standard.

To date there have been four major versions of the HTML standard. HTML 1.0 had been superseded by HTML 2.0 before most people were aware of the Web. HTML 3.0, introduced in 1995, with its later upgrade 3.2, added tables and frames, giving Web page designers much more control over layout. Until recently, 3.2 has been the working standard. We are now onto HTML 4.0, and since Internet Explorer 4.0 (IE 4.0) and Netscape Navigator 4.0 they have been built round this. IE is now on version 5.4, and Netscape has reached 6.0, but HTML seems to be sticking at 4.0 for the time being. (Which is just as well for us, as we don't want to have to completely rewrite this book for a little while yet!)

Until HTML 4.0, the changes to the standard have been incremental – new features have been added. It is only in this latest version that we have seen the introduction of features which are designed to *replace* existing ones, and even then the old features are still supported.

# HTML and browsers

For anyone writing HTML, the implications are this:

- If you want as many people as possible to be able to view your pages, in the way that you designed them, you must only use those features that are supported by all browsers. In theory, this means going back to HTML 2.0 (or even 1.0), but that would be overdoing it. I think it's fair enough to assume that the vast majority of Internet users will have at least upgraded to Netscape/IE 3.0 – so the base standard is HTML 3.2.

- If you use Microsoft or Netscape extensions that are not supported by the rival, people using the 'wrong' browser will not be able to see these when they view your pages. You can encourage visitors to change to the 'right' browser by adding '*This page looks best in Netscape/Internet Explorer*' with a link to the appropriate site so that they can download it. Both companies are very happy to cooperate on this and will supply pretty buttons, the relevant URLs and full instructions – find out more at **www.microsoft.com** and **www.netscape.com**.

- If you simply want to produce the best pages that you can, and are not too worried about how many people will be able to see them in their full glory, then make full use of HTML 4.0's possibilities – you can always add a '*Download Netscape/IE 4.0*' button.

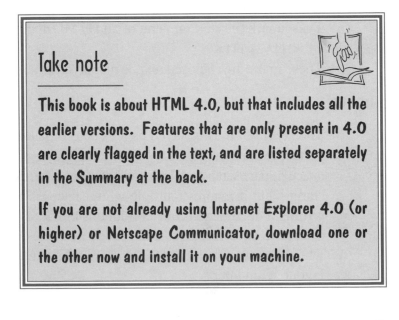

**Take note**

This book is about HTML 4.0, but that includes all the earlier versions. Features that are only present in 4.0 are clearly flagged in the text, and are listed separately in the Summary at the back.

If you are not already using Internet Explorer 4.0 (or higher) or Netscape Communicator, download one or the other now and install it on your machine.

# HTML documents

An HTML document is a text file that contains tags – code words – which can be interpreted by a browser. It must follow certain simple rules in the way that it is structured, and the tags must, of course, be written correctly, but it is otherwise a plain ASCII text file. What makes it an HTML file are its tags, and its **.HTM** or **.HTML** filename extension. (**.HTML** on Unix computers, which can cope with any length of filenames; **.HTM** was introduced for use with DOS and Windows 3.1. In Windows 95/98 you can use either.)

## The structure

A normal HTML document is divided into two sections:

- The **HEAD** contains information about the page – its author, title, keywords for search engines and the like. None of this is visible in the browser window (though the title will appear in the title bar).
- The **BODY** contains the text and links to images and other data that will be displayed in the browser.

## The tags

All tags are written in <angle brackets>. Most are written in pairs, one at either end of the text that is being formatted. Closing tags are identical to their opening tags, except that they start with a forward slash (/), e.g.

```
<HTML>  </HTML>
```

These mark the start and end of an HTML document.

```
<H1>  </H1>
```

These make the enclosed text be displayed as a level 1 heading (Chapter 2).

## Code layout

The layout of the displayed page is determined by the tags, not by the way you write the source code. When the browser reads the file, it looks for 'white space' (spaces, tabs and line breaks) to see where one word ends and the next starts – but it ignores multiple white spaces. There is nothing to stop you writing a document as one continuous block of text – except that it will be awful to read! Aim for readable code – new lines for new items, and indented where you want to identify a block within an element. We'll come back to layout again later.

# Document structure

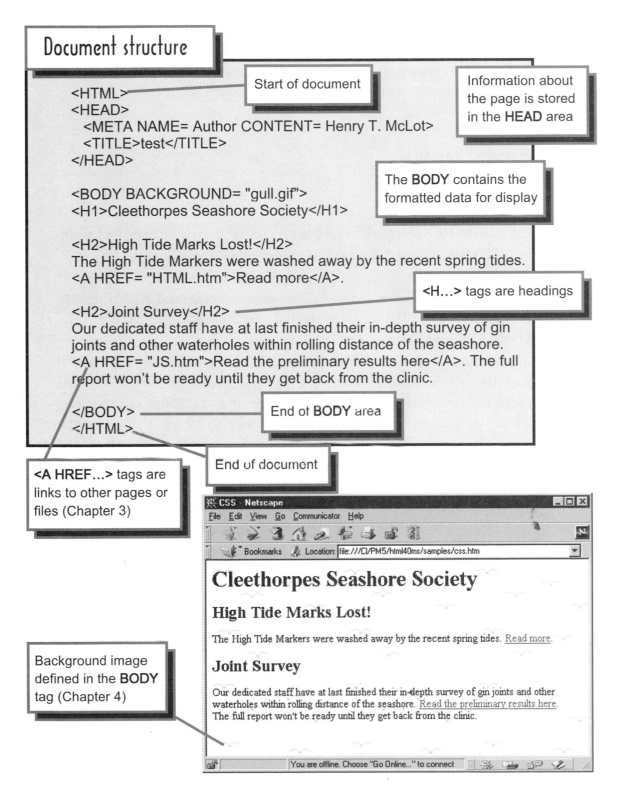

```
<HTML>
<HEAD>
  <META NAME= Author CONTENT= Henry T. McLot>
  <TITLE>test</TITLE>
</HEAD>

<BODY BACKGROUND= "gull.gif">
<H1>Cleethorpes Seashore Society</H1>

<H2>High Tide Marks Lost!</H2>
The High Tide Markers were washed away by the recent spring tides.
<A HREF= "HTML.htm">Read more</A>.

<H2>Joint Survey</H2>
Our dedicated staff have at last finished their in-depth survey of gin
joints and other waterholes within rolling distance of the seashore.
<A HREF= "JS.htm">Read the preliminary results here</A>. The full
report won't be ready until they get back from the clinic.

</BODY>
</HTML>
```

Start of document

Information about the page is stored in the **HEAD** area

The **BODY** contains the formatted data for display

**<H…>** tags are headings

End of **BODY** area

End of document

**<A HREF…>** tags are links to other pages or files (Chapter 3)

Background image defined in the **BODY** tag (Chapter 4)

---

CSS - Netscape

File  Edit  View  Go  Communicator  Help

Bookmarks    Location: file:///C|/PM5/html40ms/samples/css.htm

# Cleethorpes Seashore Society

## High Tide Marks Lost!

The High Tide Markers were washed away by the recent spring tides. Read more.

## Joint Survey

Our dedicated staff have at last finished their in-depth survey of gin joints and other waterholes within rolling distance of the seashore. Read the preliminary results here. The full report won't be ready until they get back from the clinic.

You are offline. Choose "Go Online..." to connect

# Key concepts

Let's have a closer look at that first example, as it shows some of the most important tags and some of the key concepts of HTML.

## Structure tags

**<HTML> </HTML>**

Enclose the text of the document.

**<HEAD> </HEAD>**

Enclose the HEAD area. There are several tags can be used here, including:

**<TITLE>** … page title … **</TITLE>**

The TITLE text will appear in the Title bar of the browser when the page is viewed. It will also be picked up by some search engines and used to identify the page (see page 172 for more on this).

**<META NAME = … CONTENT = …>**

**<META …>** can be used to place labelled information in the page. We'll look at the details of how it works in Chapter 10. At this point, it is the nature of the tag which is interesting. There is more to this tag than just one code word – it takes *parameters*, which pass values into the tag. In this case the parameters are **NAME**, which identifies the nature of the information, and **CONTENT**, which is the information. Notice also that this tag stands alone – it has no closing tag.

**<BODY> </BODY>**

Another essential pair of tags, these enclose the **BODY** area. In the example on page 5, the **<BODY>** tag was used with the parameter **BACKGROUND**. This is one of many options and is used here to set a background image.

**<BODY BACKGROUND= "gull.gif">**

**<BODY>** can also take options to set colours for the page. We'll return to background images in Chapter 4 and explore the other options in Chapter 2.

## Text

Plain text requires no formatting tags. Browsers will render it in whatever their default text setting may be (normally Times New Roman at 12 point), and display it as continuous text, going up to the right edge of the browser

**6**

window, wherever that may be, then wrapping round to the next line. As you'll remember from the comments on code layout (page 4), when a browser meets any amount of white space between words, it converts it into a single space in the display. For example, this code:

```
one
two                        three
four            five                    six
seven eight nine
```

produces this display (unless you use special formatting tags).

one two three four five six seven eight nine

# Text styles

Text can be formatted in several different ways, but the simplest is to use ready-made style tags. There are about a score of these, including a set for defining headings – you can see two of these in the example:

```
<H1>Cleethorpes Seashore Society</H1>
<H2>High Tide Marks Lost!</H2>
```

Text formatting is covered in Chapters 2 and 6.

# Links

Links within pages, between pages at a site and between different sites are what makes the World Wide Web. Links, or hypertext references (**HREF**) are written as parameters within anchor **<A>** tags that set them within the page. This line

```
<A HREF= "HTML.htm" >Read more</A>.
```

creates a hypertext link so that clicking on the words 'Read more' takes you to a document called "HTML.htm". Links are the subject of Chapter 3.

## Take note

Tags and other keywords can be written in upper or lower case. Capitals are used throughout this book simply to make the words more obvious.

# Writing HTML

As HTML documents are simply text files, you can create them in any text editor or word-processor. Windows 95/98 users have a choice of two suitable applications.

## Notepad

This has the key advantage of being a small, simple program. It is therefore fast to load and takes up little space in memory – an important consideration when you are likely to be running a browser (to test the display), graphics software and perhaps other applications at the same time. It only saves files as plain text, so you don't have to think about this.

There are a couple of minor disadvantages to Notepad. There's a limit to the size of file that it can handle, though as this is around 60Kb, Notepad can probably cope with any HTML pages you are likely to produce. The other catch is that it can only handle one file at a time, and it does not add recently used files to its File menu – and this is a nuisance if you are developing a set of pages and are switching backwards and forwards between them.

## WordPad

This normally works in Word format, and has many of the same formatting controls – all of which should be ignored – but will happily save and open text files. (The illustrations opposite show how to save HTML documents from WordPad.)

Though larger than Notepad, WordPad is still far more economical on resources and faster to load than a full-blown word-processor. File size is not an issue – I've yet to find an HTML document that it couldn't handle.

WordPad will not let you open several documents at once – one advantage of a word-processor for HTML work – but it does add the most recently used documents to its File menu, from where they can be easily reopened.

If I want to write or edit HTML code, I use WordPad. But this is not the only way – and not always the best way – to produce Web pages. In the next few pages we'll have a look at some alternatives.

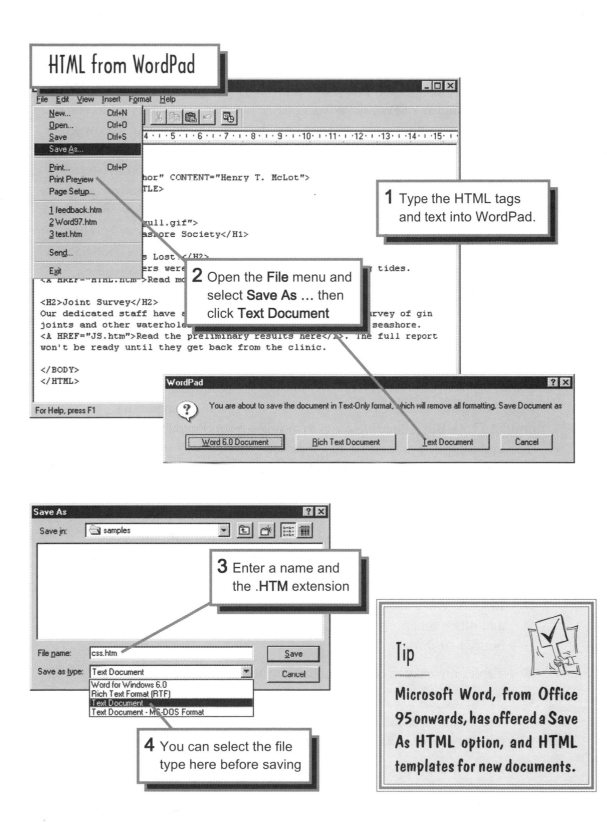

# HTML from WordPad

**1** Type the HTML tags and text into WordPad.

**2** Open the **File** menu and select **Save As ...** then click **Text Document**

WordPad

You are about to save the document in Text-Only format, which will remove all formatting. Save Document as

| Word 6.0 Document | Rich Text Document | Text Document | Cancel |

**3** Enter a name and the **.HTM** extension

File name: css.htm

Save as type: Text Document

Word for Windows 6.0
Rich Text Format (RTF)
Text Document
Text Document - MS-DOS Format

**4** You can select the file type here before saving

## Tip

Microsoft Word, from Office 95 onwards, has offered a **Save As HTML** option, and HTML templates for new documents.

# HTML editors

An HTML editor is an application specifically designed for creating Web pages. Most are WYSIWYG (What You See Is What You Get) systems – the screen display is (almost) identical to how the page will appear in a browser. The files that they produce are, of course, standard HTML source code documents. Most, including the ones introduced here, are soon mastered. You can learn to use these, at a basic level, in minutes, and become an expert with a couple of days' practice. In fact, if you only want to quickly knock up some bright and breezy Web pages, and aren't interested in why and how they work, then you could just get yourself an editor and stick this book back on the shelf! But you want to do the job properly, don't you, so read on.

Let's start by looking at FrontPage, which nicely demonstrates what you can expect from a good HTML editor.

## FrontPage

FrontPage is a fully-fledged HTML editing and Web site management suite from Microsoft, and one of the best on the market. It's also not that cheap – around £150. But it does have a baby brother, FrontPage Express, which is free and supplied as part of the Internet Explorer 4.0 package. It lacks FrontPage's site management facilities, but has virtually all of the same range of editing features. Anything that is demonstrated in this book with FrontPage, can be done equally well with FrontPage Express.

- Text is formatted in the usual way, using the toolbar buttons or options on the **Format** menu, and you can either type the text, then select it and format it, or set the format and then type your text.

- Images, video and sound clips, hyperlinks, animations, Java applets and other enhancements can be inserted either from the toolbar buttons or through the **Insert** menu.

- Tables are easy to create, and easy to format.

- There are good text-editing facilities – including 'find and replace' and a spell-checker. If necessary – and it often is – you can view and edit the HTML source code created by FrontPage.

- And when the page is done, there's a wizard to simplify the business of uploading the files to your Web space.

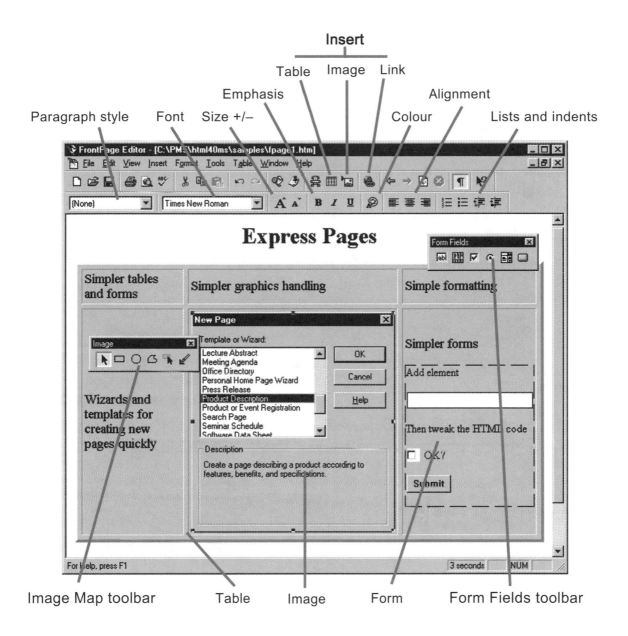

**Insert**

Table   Image   Link

Emphasis

Paragraph style   Font   Size +/–   Colour   Alignment

Lists and indents

Image Map toolbar   Table   Image   Form   Form Fields toolbar

This screenshot demonstrates some of FrontPage's finer points.

❑ The table was created and formatted with a few button-clicks.

❑ Forms are easy to lay out, using the Form Field Toolbar – though you need an understanding of HTML to be able to use forms effectively.

❑ The central image is a shot of the New Page Wizard, which can get you off to a flying start – as long as you want a page built to one of the available templates (FrontPage Express has a limited range).

❑ Any image can be used as the basis of an image map (page 66).

# Composer

Netscape Composer is supplied as part of the (free) Communicator package. It's a good editor with a similar range of features to FrontPage Express – the difference are minor:

- there are some extra text formatting tools;
- it links to your choice of word-processor to edit the source code, while FrontPage has its own built-in editor for this;
- it can't handle form fields;
- templates and wizards for creating new pages are not supplied with the software, but are available online, along with lots of support and other goodies at Netscape's Web site.

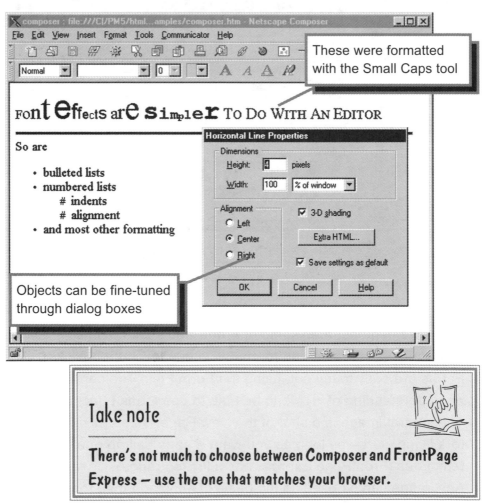

These were formatted with the Small Caps tool

Objects can be fine-tuned through dialog boxes

## Take note

There's not much to choose between Composer and FrontPage Express – use the one that matches your browser.

# Editors and hand-coding

HTML editors are great for some jobs. Creating tables, setting colours and producing intricate text effects are very fiddly to do by hand but can be managed easily by an HTML editor. For example, look at the top line of text in the screenshot from Netscape Composer on the opposite page. Here's the code behind the first word – don't try to make sense of it, just look at the quantity! Done by hand, this would have taken you ten times as long, and you would have had lots of opportunities for typing mistakes.

```
<FONT SIZE=+1>F</FONT><FONT SIZE=+2>o</FONT><FONT
SIZE=+3>n</FONT><FONT SIZE=+4>t</FONT>
```

It's with tables that you really appreciate editors. Here is the code generated by FrontPage for the first row of the table on page 11. Count those tags!

```
<TABLE BORDER="4" CELLPADDING="3" CELLSPACING="6"
BGCOLOR="#C0C0C0">
   <TR>
     <TD><FONT SIZE="4">Simpler tables and forms</FONT></TD>
     <TD><FONT SIZE="4">Simpler graphics handling</FONT></TD>
     <TD><FONT SIZE="4">Simple formatting</FONT></TD>
   </TR>
```

HTML editors have their limitations. There are some things that they cannot do for you, as you'll see when we look at forms (Chapter 7). Also, they tend to 'over-tag' – include tags which you would miss out when hand-coding. For example, in the code above, each item of text is separately enclosed by the tags **<FONT SIZE = "4"> ... </FONT>**, when one pair, at the start and end of all the text, would have done the job. They also put quotes round all values, when they are only necessary around text that contains spaces. Over-tagging is not a major problem, and if you do want to tighten things up, it's simple enough to take the code into WordPad and remove the surplus tags.

**Tip**

**Once you have got to grips with HTML, use an editor to do the donkey work and the fiddly jobs, then take the source code into WordPad to tidy it and to add those elements that cannot be handled by the editor.**

13

# Useful software

A text editor or word processor to write the code and a browser to view it in are all you need to start with, but before too long you are going to want some more software. You should get an HTML editor (unless you like doing things the hard way); you'll need something to produce images – still and animated – in a suitable format for Web pages; and you may need file transfer software to upload pages to your Web space at your Internet service provider.

## Graphics software

Browsers are designed to handle images in two formats: GIF (Graphic Image Format) and JPG or JPEG (Joint Photographic Experts Group) – see pages 55 to 58 for more on graphics formats. The Paint program supplied with Windows cannot produce files in either of these formats, but there are lots of freeware, shareware and commercial applications that can do the job. Here are two – of many – that are worth investigating.

## Paint Shop Pro

This is the leading shareware graphics package. It is excellent for creating and manipulating images – they can be resized, reversed, recoloured, deformed, despeckled, filtered and even given a hot wax coating! They can also capture images from the screen, a scanner or a digital camera. Files can be opened and output in a full range of formats, including BMP, WMF, GIF and JPG – which means that you can take pictures from Paint (BMP) or clip art (usually WMF) and convert them into a suitable format for Web pages.

The current versions, from 5.0 onwards, allow you to build pictures in 'layers' – separate background, foreground (and middle grounds) images – which can be moved and edited independently of the rest. This does not just add flexibility to your normal graphics work, it also makes it far simpler to produce sequences of related images for animations. Which brings me to Animation Shop, supplied as part of the package. This is for constructing and editing animated GIFs – one of the simplest ways to bring a bit of action to your Web pages (see page 146 for more on these).

Find out more about Paint Shop Pro at the developer's Web site:

http://www.jasc.com

Paint Shop Pro (above) showing one of their sample images. The 'wolf' is a separate layer, and so can be easily copied, moved or removed.

An animated GIF is a sequence of images, stored as one file. With Animation Shop (right) you can create the images, as well as set the timing and order of the display (see page 146 for more on this).

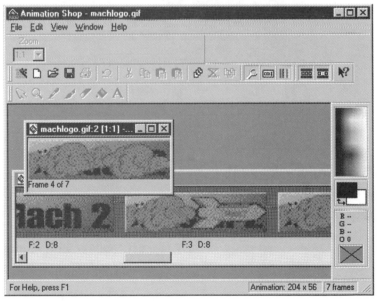

15

# Image Composer

If you are used to working with Paint, or similar graphics programs where images are created by painting lines and shapes on a 'canvas', Image Composer will be a bit of a culture shock. Each line, each shape, each block of text is a separate element or 'sprite', and these can be individually moved, manipulated and have colour or surface effects applied to them. The sprites can then be arranged and overlaid to create the desired effect.

Image Composer is supplied as part of the full FrontPage package, but can also be obtained from the Microsoft Developer Network Web site at:

http://msdn.microsoft.com/developer/

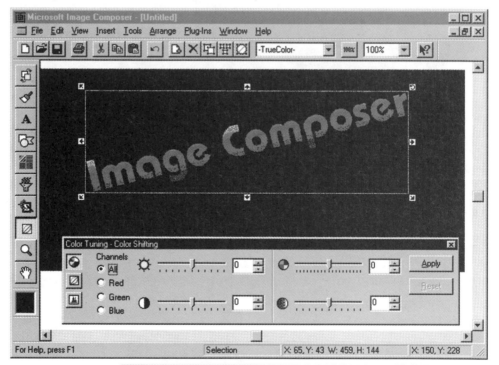

There are two sprites in the screenshot – the text and the patterened background.

## Take note

You must register with Microsoft Developer Network before you can download software or use the other services at the site, but registration is free.

# GIF animator

This is far simpler than Animation Shop, but very easy to use. Just give it a set of images (perhaps created in Image Composer), set the order and the timing, and it will turn them into an animated GIF.

GIF Animator is also available from the Microsoft Developers Network.

There's more on animated GIFs on page 146

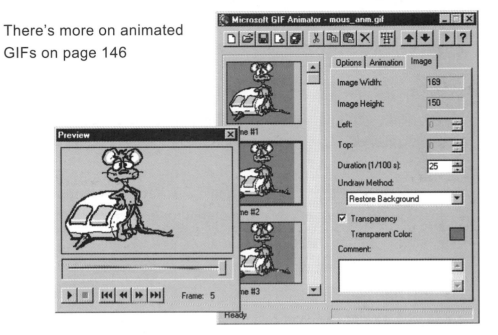

# WS_FTP

FTP stands for File Transfer Protocol and is the standard method for copying files across the Internet. Both Microsoft and Netscape offer Web Publishing Wizards to handle uploading your pages to your Web site, and both do the job very efficiently – though adding a few odd pages to an existing site can be fiddly, and neither will let you remove unwanted pages. If you don't have a wizard, or you want more control over the contents of your Web space, you will need an FTP program. WS_FTP is the leading file transfer program, and is free for educational and personal use. We'll have a look at using WS_FTP for uploading your files in Chapter 10.

# Summary

❑　HTML is a coding system that tells browsers how to interpret and display Web pages. The system has developed over the last few years. Version 3.2 is currently the most widely used, but is being superseded by HTML 4.0.

❑　You need a modern browser to get the best out of HTML. You should have at least version 4.0 of either Internet Explorer or Netscape Navigator.

❑　HTML documents are divided into the HEAD, which contains non-displaying information about the page, and BODY, which is the displayed page. The document filename will normally have a .HTM or .HTML extension.

❑　HTML tags are written in <angle brackets>, and are normally in pairs – one at either end of the material to be formatted.

❑　You can write HTML code in any text editor or word-processor – WordPad is an excellent choice for Windows users.

❑　HTML can be written purely by hand, but editors make light work of the trickier jobs, but tend to produce ungainly code. The free and freely available FrontPage Express and Netscape Composer both have some limitations, but can handle most aspects of HTML. If you are going to create a full-blown Web site for an organisation, you'll need the advanced editing and site management facilities of FrontPage, or a similar high-level HTML suite.

❑　As well as a word-processor, HTML editor and a brower, you may also need some graphics software and WS_FTP for uploading files to your Web space.

# 2 Working with text

Plain text and headings . . . . . . . . . 20

Alignment . . . . . . . . . . . . . . . . . . 23

Text appearance . . . . . . . . . . . . . . 25

Size . . . . . . . . . . . . . . . . . . . . . . 28

Colour . . . . . . . . . . . . . . . . . . . . 29

Typefaces . . . . . . . . . . . . . . . . . . 32

Lists . . . . . . . . . . . . . . . . . . . . . . 34

Summary . . . . . . . . . . . . . . . . . . 36

# Plain text and headings

Unformatted text is normally displayed in Times New Roman, 12 point – the same as this text, though it looks a little different on screen. It is laid out as a solid block, with each word following directly after each other (separated by a single space) – no matter how you spaced out the code. When the text meets the right edge of the browser window – wherever that may be – it is wrapped to the next line. If you want your text on separate lines, you must use tags.

## <BR> Line break

The **<BR>** tag makes any following text (or image) start on a new line. This is the simplest of all tags, taking no options and having no closing tag. In normal word-processing terms, **<BR>** is the equivalent of pressing the [Enter] key once.

```
Here's a bit of text
<BR>and this is the next line.
```

When writing your code, the final layout will be more obvious if you put **<BR>** at the start of a new line.

## <P> Paragraph </P>

The **<P>** tag also moves following text to the next line, but this first creates a line space between it and the text above. **<P>** can take an optional parameter to define the alignment of the text in the paragraph, and we'll look at this later in this chapter.

The closing tag **</P>** can be omitted if the following text start with **<P>**, **<BR>** or a heading tag. It is common practice to miss them out where you have a succession of paragraphs, e.g.

```
<P>First paragraph …
<P>Second paragraph …
…
<P>Last paragraph</P>
following text
```

As a general rule, use **<P>** where you have a lot of text that you want to split into clearly marked paragraphs, and **<BR>** where text must go on separate lines but is closely related, e.g. an address, a poem, a list of items.

# <H...> Headings </H...>

The heading tags, **<H1> ... </H1>** to **<H6> ... </H6>**, display text in Times New Roman, **bold**, with a line space above and below. There are six levels of heading, with sizes normally ranging from 24 point down to 8 point.

These settings are not fixed, but depend upon the browser in which the page is being viewed. Almost all browsers allow their users to select the fonts and to increase or decrease all font sizes – however, even if the sizes are changed, they will remain the same relative to each other. You cannot guarantee that anyone viewing your page will see **<H1>** text at 24 point, but you can guarantee that it will be the biggest heading!

# <H1>Heading 1 is 24 point</H1>

## <H2>Heading 2 is 18 point</H2>

### <H3>Heading 3 is 14 point</H3>

#### <H4>Heading 4 is 12 point (same as normal)</H4>

##### <H5>Heading 5 is 10 point (and hard to read)</H5>

###### <H6>Heading 6 is 8 point (and horribly small)</H6>

All **<H...>** tags can take the same alignment options as the **<P>** tag, as you will see shortly.

# Horizontal rules

The **<HR>** tag draws a line in the current text colour. It is normally 6 pixels deep, with a 3D effect, across the full width of the window, but can be formatted by these options:

**SIZE** = sets the depth in pixels;

**WIDTH** = set either in pixels or as a percentage of the window width;

**NOSHADE** turns off the 3D effect, giving a solid line.

Examples:

```
<HR SIZE=12 WIDTH=80%>
<HR SIZE=8 WIDTH=200 NOSHADE>
```

The first draws a 3D line, 12 pixels deep across 80% or the window; the second line is 8 pixels deep by 200 wide, and in solid colour.

# Text and Headings

```
<HTML>
<HEAD>
  <TITLE>Text and Headings</TITLE>
</HEAD>
<BODY>

<H1>Hot Times in Madrid and London</H1>
This is the place to go to find the places to go!
<P>And when you get there, don't forget to tell them how you found them.

<H2>Madrid</H2>
<H3>Day Time</H3>
Plaza del Sol, in the middle away from the trees
<BR> - 11 am to 3 pm.
<H3>Night Time</H3>
Basement cells 17 to 43, Central Police Station
<BR>- no windows or air conditioning

<H2>London</H2>
Hot Times in London? You must be joking

</BODY>
</HTML>
```

**<P>** tag creates space above

**<BR>** to keep lines close together

All headings have a line space above and below

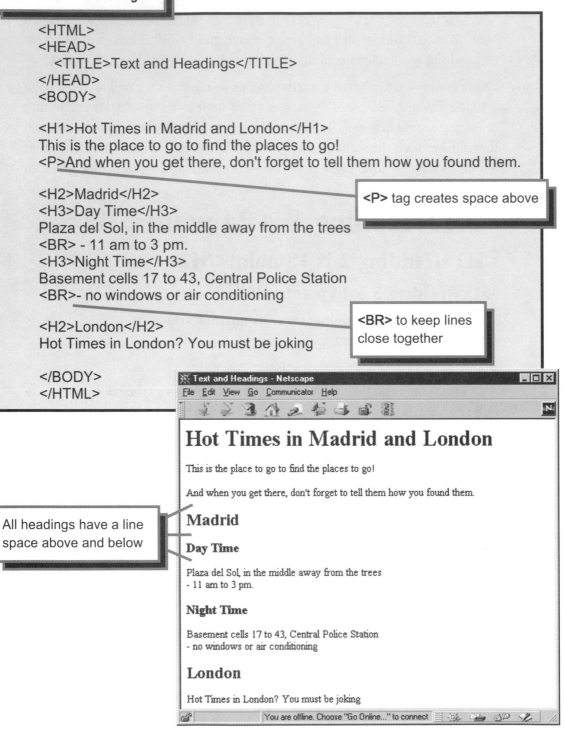

**Text and Headings - Netscape**

File  Edit  View  Go  Communicator  Help

# Hot Times in Madrid and London

This is the place to go to find the places to go!

And when you get there, don't forget to tell them how you found them.

## Madrid

### Day Time

Plaza del Sol, in the middle away from the trees
- 11 am to 3 pm.

### Night Time

Basement cells 17 to 43, Central Police Station
- no windows or air conditioning

## London

Hot Times in London? You must be joking

You are offline. Choose "Go Online..." to connect

# Alignment

Plain text and headings are normally displayed aligned to the left of the window, with a 'ragged' right edge. You can set the alignment to centre, right or fully justified. Actually, 'fully justified' is an optimistic description. It should mean aligning the text to both edges of the window – just as this text is aligned to both sides of the page area – but in practice, it does no more than make a brave stab at it.

Alignment can be set in several ways. The simplest is with the **ALIGN** option in the **<P>** and **<H...>** tags. The keywords are **LEFT**, **CENTER**, **RIGHT**, and **JUSTIFY**. Like all keywords in HTML, these can be written in upper or lower case, and can be enclosed in "double quotes". (You will find quotes around keywords in code generated by HTML editors; lazier humans tend to miss them out.) For examples:

```
<P ALIGN = RIGHT>This text is right-aligned</P>
<H1 ALIGN = CENTER>A centred heading</H1>
<P ALIGN = LEFT>Looks just like normal</P>
```

Try them, or try the larger example on the next page.

## <CENTER> </CENTER>

This pair of tags set centre alignment as the default for all text and images enclosed by them. Within these tags, paragraphs and headings can be aligned separately, but it will switch back to centred after the closing **</P>** or **<H...>**.

Other alignments can be set as the default for a section using the **<DIV>** tag, but let's leave that until later (page 115) as it raises other issues.

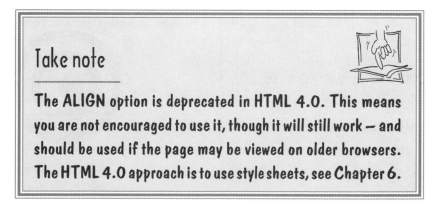

**Take note**

The ALIGN option is deprecated in HTML 4.0. This means you are not encouraged to use it, though it will still work – and should be used if the page may be viewed on older browsers. The HTML 4.0 approach is to use style sheets, see Chapter 6.

## Alignment

```
<HTML>
<HEAD>
  <TITLE>Alignment</TITLE>
</HEAD>
<BODY>

<H1 ALIGN = CENTER>How To Modify Layout</H1>

Align to left (normal)
<P ALIGN = CENTER>Set in the centre, but spell it CENTER</P>

<P ALIGN=RIGHT>Align on the right</P>

<CENTER>
    You can set the alignment to affect all subsequent text and graphics
    <BR><IMG SRC="target.gif">
    <P ALIGN = LEFT> A bit on the side</P>
    and back to the centre
</CENTER>
</BODY>
</HTML>
```

Sets the alignment within this heading only

Everything centred until switched off by **</CENTER>**

Notice the **<BR>** and **<P>** to set the image and text onto separate lines

Lines indented to show the centred section more clearly

### Take note

HTML 4.0 supports the use of style sheets, which allow you to redefine the formats of the ‹P› and ‹H ..› – and most other – tags. See Chapter 6.

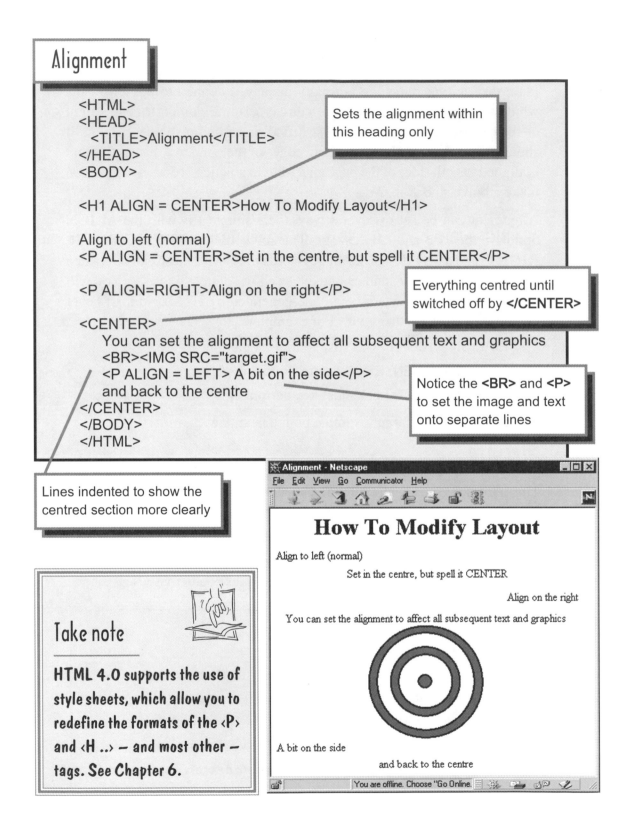

Alignment - Netscape
File  Edit  View  Go  Communicator  Help

# How To Modify Layout

Align to left (normal)

Set in the centre, but spell it CENTER

Align on the right

You can set the alignment to affect all subsequent text and graphics

A bit on the side

and back to the centre

You are offline. Choose "Go Online.

# Text appearance

## Font styles

These modify the appearance of text – and of headings.

| Tags | Effect |
|------|--------|
| <B> </B> | **bold** |
| <I> </I> | *italic* |
| <TT></TT> | `TypewriTer (Courier New)` |
| <BIG> </BIG> | 2 points bigger than normal |
| <SMALL> </SMALL> | 2 point smaller than normal |
| <SUB> </SUB> | $_{Sub}$script |
| <SUP> </SUP> | $^{Super}$script |

The tags can be used to pick out text within paragraphs and headings, or can enclose a larger section of code, contain other formatting tags – though some effects may cancel out others. They must be written in pairs, and must always be properly 'nested' – i.e. the first tag to close is the last that was opened.

   <B>This is <I>very</I> important.</B>

is displayed as:

   **This is *very* important.**

If you are using tags to modify the style of headings, they must be within – not outside – **<H...>** tags.  Written outside, they have no effect.

   <H3><TT>from my t<I>rusty</I> typewriter</TT></H3>

is displayed as:

   `from my `*`trusty`*` typewriter`

This is still a 14 point heading, but now in Courier, with 'rusty' in italics.

## Phrasal elements

The tags in this set also affect the appearance of the text, but are really intended for marking up documents for analysis by search routines or other programs. If you are only concerned with the display, use **<B>**, **<I>** or **<TT>**.

The tags are covered in the section *Tags and Options* (page 182) – their effects are illustrated in the screenshot overleaf.

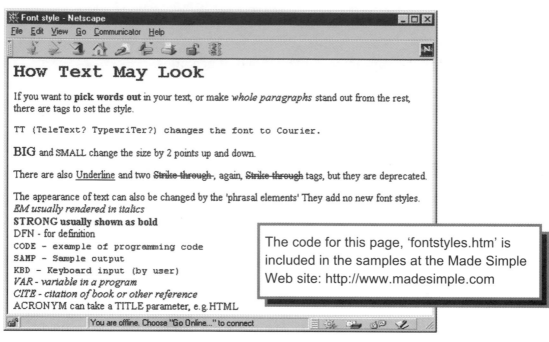

## <ADDRESS> </ADDRESS>

This is conventionally used to enclose the author's contact details and date of the last update to page, and normally appears at the bottom of the home page of a site. It starts text on a new line, and displays it in italics. If you want several lines of details, enclose them in one **<ADDRESS>...</ADDRESS>** pair, and separate the lines with **<BR>** tags.

## <BLOCKQUOTE> </BLOCKQUOTE>

This tag sets the layout, rather than the style, and is intended for displaying multi-line quotes. Text is shown in the normal font, but is indented from the left, and with a line space above and below. If separate lines or paragraphs are needed within the block, use **<BR>** or **<P>** as normal.

```
<BLOCKQUOTE>"Plagiarize,
<BR>Let no one else's work evade your eyes"</BLOCKQUOTE>
```

From Lobachevsky by Tom Lehrer (and I've acknowledged it!)

# <PRE> Pre-formatted text</PRE>

This tag overrules the normal treatment of white space. Text written inside **<PRE>...</PRE>** tags is displayed with the spaces, tabs and new lines exactly as they were written in the code. Use it for poems, special text effects and other situations where carefully spaced layout is required.

Other formatting tags can be written within **<PRE>...</PRE>** – but remember that the space they occupy in the code will disappear on screen.

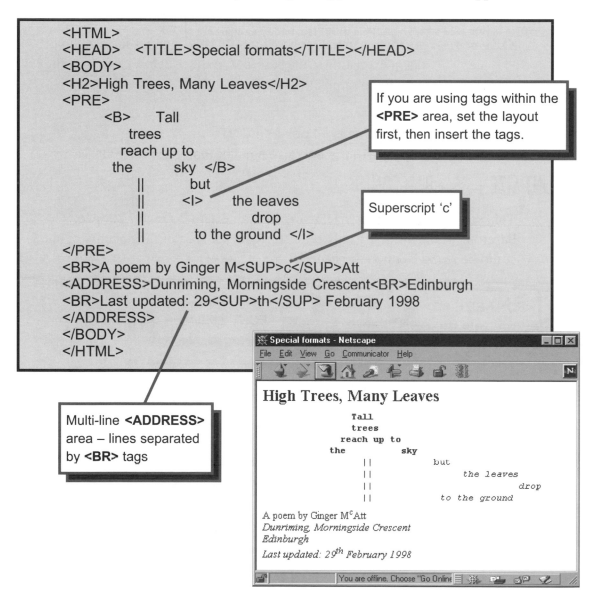

```
<HTML>
<HEAD>   <TITLE>Special formats</TITLE></HEAD>
<BODY>
<H2>High Trees, Many Leaves</H2>
<PRE>
      <B>    Tall
          trees
        reach up to
     the       sky </B>
        ||         but
        ||    <I>     the leaves
        ||              drop
        ||        to the ground  </I>
</PRE>
<BR>A poem by Ginger M<SUP>c</SUP>Att
<ADDRESS>Dunriming, Morningside Crescent<BR>Edinburgh
<BR>Last updated: 29<SUP>th</SUP> February 1998
</ADDRESS>
</BODY>
</HTML>
```

If you are using tags within the **<PRE>** area, set the layout first, then insert the tags.

Superscript 'c'

Multi-line **<ADDRESS>** area – lines separated by **<BR>** tags

**Special formats - Netscape**

File  Edit  View  Go  Communicator  Help

## High Trees, Many Leaves

```
            Tall
            trees
          reach up to
       the           sky
            ||              but
            ||                    the leaves
            ||                           drop
            ||              to the ground
```

A poem by Ginger M$^c$Att
*Dunriming, Morningside Crescent*
*Edinburgh*
*Last updated: 29$^{th}$ February 1998*

You are offline. Choose "Go Online

# Size

## <FONT SIZE = > </FONT>

The **<FONT ...>** tag can be used to set the size, colour and typeface of text. Size can be set in two ways:

**SIZE = n**    where $n$ is from 1 to 7, and each value has a fixed size. The sizes are 1 = 8 point; 2 = 10 point; 3 = 12 point; 4 = 14 point; 5 = 18 point; 6 = 24 point; 7 = 36 point.

**SIZE = +/–n**    where $n$ is in the range –4 to +4. This changes the size up or down in relation to the basefont size (see below), but working within the same 8 to 36 point range.

Examples:

<FONT SIZE = 4>This is 14 point </FONT>

<FONT SIZE = -1>This is one size smaller than normal</FONT>

## <BASEFONT SIZE = > <BASEFONT>

This sets the default font size, using the same 1 to 7 range as above. The basefont would normally only be set once, at the start of the document, but could be resent as often as needed.

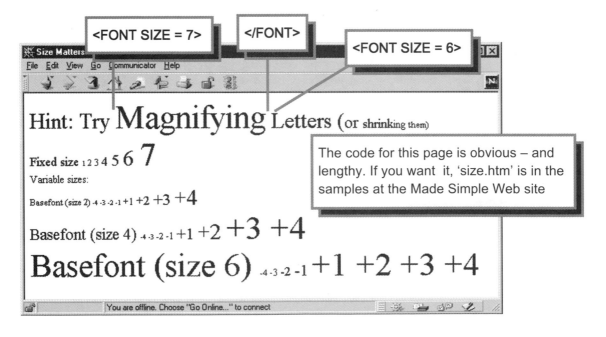

28

# Colour

The colour of the page background and default colours for text can be set in the <**BODY**> tag; the colour of selected blocks of text can be set in <**FONT**> tags. Colours are always defined in the same ways – either using colour names or hexadecimal values. Colour names give you a limited (though adequate) range – only 16 names are recognised. Using hexadecimal values you can specify colours exactly from a palette of 24 million colours! (But it's worth remembering that many people use a 256-colour display.)

Hexadecimal colour values look awful at first glance, but are quickly mastered once you understand the basic pattern.

## Instant Hex

All modern numbering systems are founded on 'place value' – how much a digit stands for depends upon its place in the figure. 42 means $4 \times 10 + 2$. In hexadecimal, the place value multiplicr is 16, rather than 10. So, 42 in hexadecimal is worth $4 \times 16 + 2$ (= 66 in the normal, base-10 system). To make this work, more digits are needed – 0 1 2 3 4 5 6 7 8 9 A B C D E F – with A to F standing for 10 to 15 in the base-10 system.

Hexadecimal is used in computing because it is very compact – you can represent any value between 0 and 255 with two hex digits ($FF = 15 \times 16 + 15 = 255$) – and there is a simple conversion between hex and binary, the native system of computer chips. (Believe me, converting base-10 to binary is a chore; hex to binary a piece of cake.)

## RGB colours

All colours on a screen are creating by combining red, green and blue light in varying intensities. For example, bright red and bright green produce yellow; add bright blue and you have white; half-power red and blue give a deep purple. The intensity of each colour can be set on a scale of 0 to 255 – or rather, 00 to FF, as hexadecimal values are used.

In HTML, as in most computing systems, the values are given in the order red, green, blue. For example, FF0080 means red at full power, no green and blue at half power; 808080 sets all three at half power and gives you grey. The values are normally written with # at the start, to indicate that they are hexadecimal. They can be enclosed in quotes, but this is purely optional.

## The standard colour set

| Colour name | Hex value R G B | Colour name | Hex value R G B |
|---|---|---|---|
| Black | #000000 | Green | #008000 |
| Silver | #C0C0C0 | Lime | #00FF00 |
| Gray * | #808080 | Olive | #808000 |
| White | #FFFFFF | Yellow | #FFFF00 |
| Maroon | #800000 | Navy | #000080 |
| Red | #FF0000 | Blue | #0000FF |
| Purple | #800080 | Teal | #008080 |
| Fuchsia | #FF00FF | Aqua | #00FFFF |

\* N.B. American spelling

## &lt;BODY&gt; colours

These options in the **&lt;BODY&gt;** tag can be used to set the colour of the background, and of the normal and link text.

| | |
|---|---|
| BGCOLOR = | background |
| TEXT = | normal text |
| LINK = | link not yet visited |
| VLINK = | visited link |
| ALINK = | current link |

For example, to set a yellow page background with navy text and unvisited links in red (but leaving other link colours at their defaults) you would use:

&lt;BODY BGCOLOR= Yellow TEXT = Navy LINK = Red&gt;
*or*  &lt;BODY BGCOLOR= #FFFF00 TEXT = #000080 LINK = #FF000&gt;

## &lt;FONT COLOR = &gt;

Selected text within a page can be coloured using the **COLOR** option within **&lt;FONT&gt;** tags. The colour is used until changed by another **&lt;FONT COLOR = …&gt;** tag, or turned off with **&lt;/FONT&gt;**.

Note that **COLOR**, **BGCOLOR** and every other colour-setting option in HTML uses the American spelling.

## Colours

```
<HTML>
<HEAD>
  <TITLE>Colours</TITLE>
</HEAD>

<BODY TEXT=Magenta BGCOLOR=Lime LINK=Navy VLINK=Blue
ALINK=Red>

<CENTER>
<H1><FONT COLOR=Purple>Helpful Tips for Modern Ladies</FONT></H1>

<H2><FONT COLOR=Teal>No 437: Colour Co-ordination</FONT></H2>
 </CENTER>
 <B>
 <FONT COLOR=#FF8080 SIZE=+2>Pink</FONT>

<P>Pink is this year's <FONT COLOR=Black>black</FONT>!
Everyone should have a little pink dress in their walk-in wardrobe.

<P><FONT COLOR=#FF00FF>Be <FONT COLOR=#FF00CC>daring
<FONT COLOR=#FF0080>with <FONT COLOR=#800080>your <FONT
COLOR=#8000FF>colour <FONT COLOR=#4000FF>mixes! </FONT>
 </B>
 </BODY>
 </HTML>
```

Set background and default text colours for whole page

**<FONT COLOR =...>** also applies to headings

Hex values let you mix your own colours

**</FONT>** can be omitted before another **<FONT COLOR =...>** tag

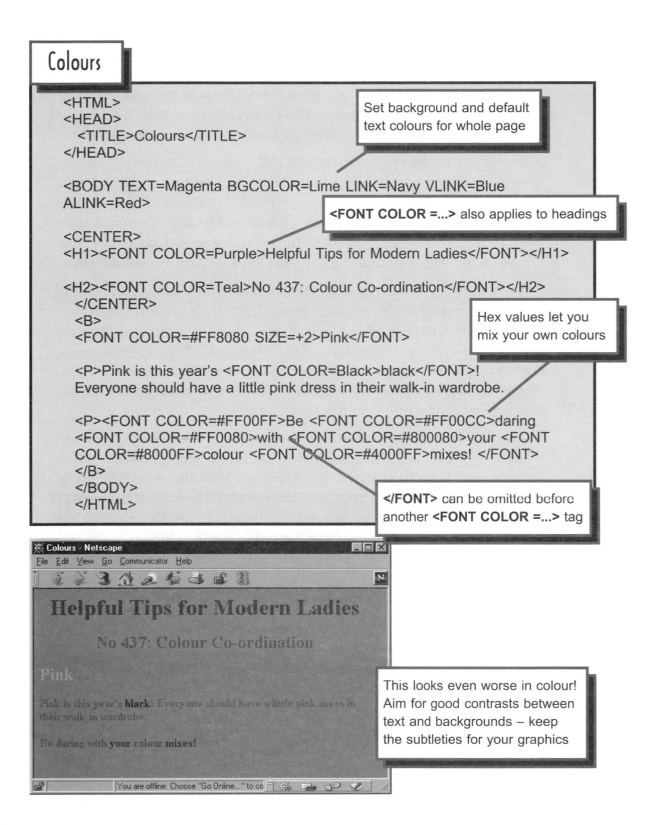

## Helpful Tips for Modern Ladies

### No 437: Colour Co-ordination

**Pink**

Pink is this year's **black**! Everyone should have a little pink dress in their walk-in wardrobe.

Be daring with **your colour mixes!**

This looks even worse in colour! Aim for good contrasts between text and backgrounds – keep the subtleties for your graphics

# Typefaces

The **<FONT ...>** tag has a third option – **FACE** – which lets you select the typeface, or font name. Though, in theory, this gives you great flexibility in your text displays, in practice there are problems and no simple solutions.

The root cause of the problems is that HTML does not carry font information within its own system. Instead, it normally relies on the fonts that exist within the computer on which a page is being viewed. If you are publishing only on an intranet – within an organisation – you should be able to ensure that the required fonts are present on all machines. But if you are publishing your page on the Web, you cannot know what fonts all your readers will have.

Anyone running Windows (about 90% of all users) will have a small core of common fonts: Arial, Courier New, Σψμβολ (Symbol), Times New Roman and ☯✴■♈♒♎✴■♈♒◆ (Wingdings). Those fonts that are distributed with Word and Works are probably also present on most Windows machines, but you have no guarantee of these – and unless you have only recently set up your machine, or are very methodical, you almost certainly won't be able to remember where all your fonts came from!

It is possible to embed fonts into your pages, but it's hard work. Microsoft has developed a font embedding system for its browsers – the WEFT (Web Embedding Font Tool) is available from their Web site. After some early work, Netscape seems to have decided that font embedding is not the way forward. They did offer an embedding tool for use with Netscape 4.0, but have abandonned it altogether with Netscape 6.0. The *font family* attribute in style sheets (see page 104) is fully implemented by all newer browsers and gives you a good degree of control over the choice of fonts, without the download overhead of embedding them.

If you want to pursue this path, you can find out more by looking for 'graphics font' at Webmonkey:

http://www.hotwired.com/webmonkey/

## Font faces

```
<HTML>
<HEAD>
    <TITLE>Font faces</TITLE>
</HEAD>

<BODY>
<H1>HoT MetaL</H1>
<BASEFONT SIZE = 4>
20 years ago, printers used Hot Metal technology; soon they will use HTML.
<P>There are thousands of font faces, falling into three groups

<P><FONT FACE = Arial>
Sans serif - meaning no twiddly bits, like this (Arial)

<P><FONT FACE = "Century Schoolbook">
Serif - little tails on the long strokes, like this (Century Schoolbook)
</FONT>

<P>Display fonts - for special effects. Examples:
<BR><FONT FACE = "Comic Sans MS">
Comic Sans MS
<BR><FONT FACE = "Lucida Calligraphy">Lucida Calligraphy
<BR><FONT FACE = "Impact">Impact</FONT>
</BASEFONT>
</BODY>
</HTML>
```

As there is no **</FONT>** tag here, the font reverts to Arial after the next **</FONT>**

Choose your own fonts – but remember that only the Windows core fonts are widely available.

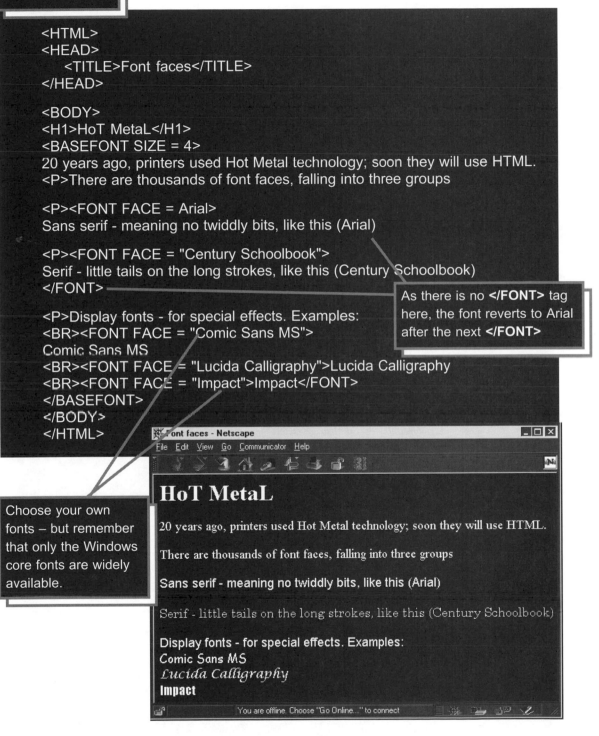

**HoT MetaL**

20 years ago, printers used Hot Metal technology; soon they will use HTML.

There are thousands of font faces, falling into three groups

Sans serif - meaning no twiddly bits, like this (Arial)

Serif - little tails on the long strokes, like this (Century Schoolbook)

Display fonts - for special effects. Examples:
Comic Sans MS
Lucida Calligraphy
Impact

33

# Lists

## Unordered (bulleted) list

The list is enclosed with **<UL>...</UL>** tags, with an option, **TYPE**, to define the bullets. These can be **DISC** •, **CIRCLE** ○ and **SQUARE** .

Each item in the list is marked by **<LI>** at the start. The closing **</LI>** tag is optional, and normally omitted.

## Ordered (numbered) list

Here the main list tags are **<OL>...</OL>**. **<OL>** also has a **TYPE** option, which in this case specifies the numbering system: **1** (numbers), **A** or **a** (upper or lower case letters), **I** or **i** (upper or lower case Roman numerals). It can also take a **START =** option, which gives the starting value for the list. This value must always be given as a number, whatever the **TYPE** style.

Ordered list items again use the **<LI>...</LI>** tags. **<LI>** can take a **VALUE** option, which sets the number for the item, with any subsequent items numbered in sequence, e.g.

```
<OL>
    <LI>Aston Villa
    <LI>Manchester United
    <LI VALUE = 19>Blackburn
    <LI>Southampton
</OL>
```

The output from this is:

1. Aston Villa
2. Manchester United
19. Blackburn
20. Southampton

## Definition list

This produces a convenient layout for definitions of terms, references and similar. The list is enclosed by **<DL>...</DL>**. Each item to be defined is marked by **<DT>**; the definition by **<DD>** (the closing tags **</DT> </DD>** are optional). Apart from indenting the definition, no formatting is applied.

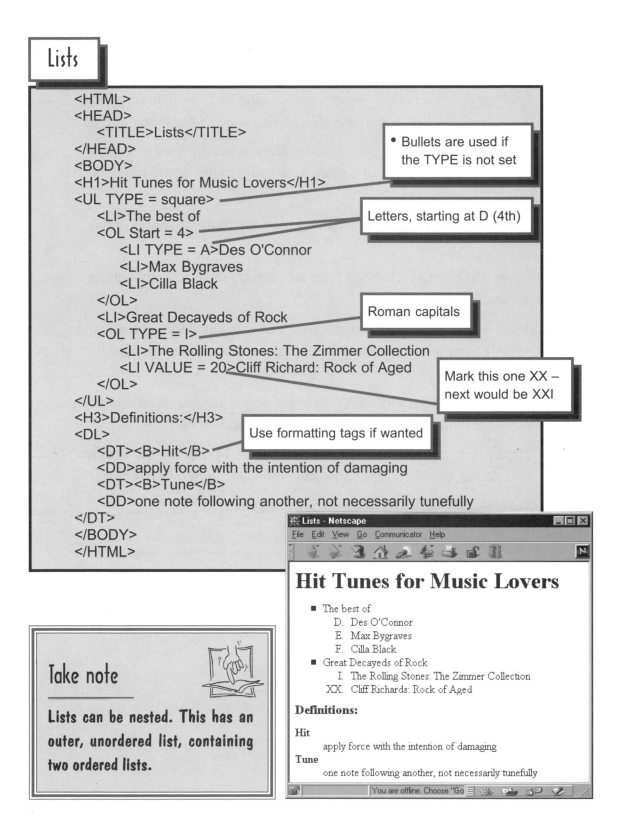

```
<HTML>
<HEAD>
    <TITLE>Lists</TITLE>
</HEAD>
<BODY>
<H1>Hit Tunes for Music Lovers</H1>
<UL TYPE = square>
    <LI>The best of
    <OL Start = 4>
        <LI TYPE = A>Des O'Connor
        <LI>Max Bygraves
        <LI>Cilla Black
    </OL>
    <LI>Great Decayeds of Rock
    <OL TYPE = I>
        <LI>The Rolling Stones: The Zimmer Collection
        <LI VALUE = 20>Cliff Richard: Rock of Aged
    </OL>
</UL>
<H3>Definitions:</H3>
<DL>
    <DT><B>Hit</B>
    <DD>apply force with the intention of damaging
    <DT><B>Tune</B>
    <DD>one note following another, not necessarily tunefully
</DT>
</BODY>
</HTML>
```

- Bullets are used if the TYPE is not set

Letters, starting at D (4th)

Roman capitals

Mark this one XX – next would be XXI

Use formatting tags if wanted

**Take note**

Lists can be nested. This has an outer, unordered list, containing two ordered lists.

**Lists - Netscape**

File  Edit  View  Go  Communicator  Help

# Hit Tunes for Music Lovers

- The best of
    - D.  Des O'Connor
    - E.  Max Bygraves
    - F.  Cilla Black
- Great Decayeds of Rock
    - I.  The Rolling Stones: The Zimmer Collection
    - XX.  Cliff Richards: Rock of Aged

**Definitions:**

**Hit**
    apply force with the intention of damaging
**Tune**
    one note following another, not necessarily tunefully

You are offline. Choose "Go

# Summary

❑ Text is separated into lines and paragraphs by the <BR> and <P> tags. The tags <H1> to <H6> give you a range of headings.

❑ If you want to divide a page into sections, you can draw attractive horizontal rules – without adding noticeably to the download time – using the <HR> tag.

❑ Text (and images) can be aligned to the left, right or centre of the window.

❑ There are a set of font style tags that can be used to emphasise or otherwise pick out text.

❑ If you want to specify the appearance of your text more closely, the <FONT> tag takes options that let you set the size, colour and typeface.

❑ Colours are defined by using standard colour names or hexadecimal values for the RGB (Red, Green, Blue) components.

❑ Though you can use any typeface you like, in practice, it is best to stick to the standard range that everyone will have on their systems.

❑ Bulletted or numbered lists are easy to define.

# 3 Links

Hypertext . . . . . . . . . . . . . . . . . . 38

Links within a page . . . . . . . . . . . 40

Multi-page structures . . . . . . . . . . 42

Mailto: me . . . . . . . . . . . . . . . . . 46

Other links . . . . . . . . . . . . . . . . . 47

Sumary . . . . . . . . . . . . . . . . . . . 48

# Hypertext

Hypertext links are what makes HTML special – without them it would just be another display system. Links allow movement within a (long) page; between the pages at a site; to other people's pages across the Web; and to files and other resources in your site or distant ones.

Whatever the link, the same basic tag is used:

```
<A HREF = "target_URL"> linked element </A>
```

The *target_URL* is the location to jump to;  the *linked element* is the text or image that will be clicked to activate the link.

Links are generally straightforward to set up, though there are a few wrinkles that you must watch out for. The simplest links are to other Web pages.

## URLs and links across the Web

Every page, file, site and person on the Internet – not just on the World Wide Web – has an URL (Uniform Resource Locator). This defines where the resource is to be found and how to connect to it. For a link to a Web page, the URL takes the form:

```
http://domain_name/directory/page
```

http:// tells the browser to use the HyperTexT Protocol to connect to it. Different protocols are used for files, e-mail addresses and other types of resources.

domain_name is the address of the site. It will usually start with 'www' and will often incorporate the organisation's real name. Part describes its type, **com**mercial, **edu**cational (or **ac**ademic), **net**working or other **org**anisation. Outside of the US, it will normally include a country code. For example, *www.madesimple.co.uk* is Made Simple's commercial site in the UK.

directory is included if the page's file is stored in a subdirectory at the site. This may be a path down through several levels of directory (on the Web, 'folders' are called 'directories').

page is the name of the document file. It may be omitted for 'home pages' – the entry points to sites. These usually have standard names, the most common of which is *index.html*.

Examples:

    http://www.yahoo.com

    http://www.clicked.com/shareware/

    http://www.utoronto.ca/webdocs/HTMLdocs/pc_tools.html

The first is Yahoo's home page. The second is top page of the Top 20 Shareware Gallery, run by Clicked. The last is an excellent resource for HTML writers, and can be found (working right to left) in the *HTMLdocs* directory of the *webdocs* directory. at the University of Toronto in Canada.

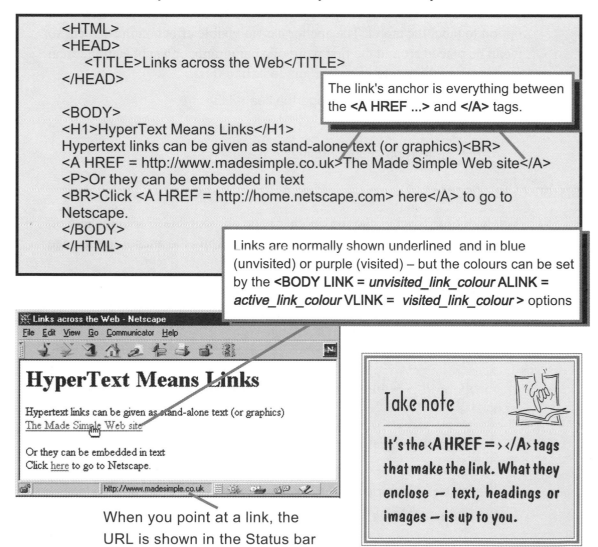

```
<HTML>
<HEAD>
    <TITLE>Links across the Web</TITLE>
</HEAD>

<BODY>
<H1>HyperText Means Links</H1>
Hypertext links can be given as stand-alone text (or graphics)<BR>
<A HREF = http://www.madesimple.co.uk>The Made Simple Web site</A>
<P>Or they can be embedded in text
<BR>Click <A HREF = http://home.netscape.com> here</A> to go to
Netscape.
</BODY>
</HTML>
```

The link's anchor is everything between the **<A HREF ...>** and **</A>** tags.

Links are normally shown underlined and in blue (unvisited) or purple (visited) – but the colours can be set by the **<BODY LINK =** *unvisited_link_colour* **ALINK =** *active_link_colour* **VLINK =** *visited_link_colour* **>** options

**Links across the Web - Netscape**

File  Edit  View  Go  Communicator  Help

# HyperText Means Links

Hypertext links can be given as stand-alone text (or graphics)
The Made Simple Web site

Or they can be embedded in text
Click here to go to Netscape.

http://www.madesimple.co.uk

When you point at a link, the URL is shown in the Status bar

Take note

It's the ‹A HREF = › ‹/A› tags that make the link. What they enclose — text, headings or images — is up to you.

39

# Links within a page

As a general rule, it's best to keep pages relatively short. If you can get your message over in a single screenful, that's ideal, and most people will happily follow a story down through a couple of screensful. Anything longer than this, and you must supply a means of navigating within the document. The solution lies in the use of anchors – target points embedded in the document. Links to these can be held in a 'contents list' at the top of the page, and this should itself be anchored so that readers can return easily to the contents to select another section.

Anchors use the same <A ...> </A> tags as links, but this time with a **NAME** option to label the target. The anchor has no visible effect on the screen, so it can be placed around the first word of a paragraph, or a subheading, or an icon – or anything you like. Anchors look like this:

```
<A NAME = opps> <H3>Opportunities </H3> </A>
```

When linking to an anchor, the URL is the anchor name, prefixed by #, e.g.

```
<A HREF = #opps>Opportunities </A>
```

## Anchors on other pages

You can jump to an anchor on another page on your site – or anywhere on the Web, as long as you know the name – by adding the anchor to the page URL. e.g.

```
<A HREF = phones.htm#GtoL> Telephone directory, G to L </A>
<A HREF = homepages.net.co.uk/~fbloggs/pets.htm#tiddles>
The biggest ginger Tom in Yorkshire</A>
```

**Tip**

Linking to anchors in other people's pages, elsewhere on the Web, is a risky business. It's bad enough linking to other sites. People move, rename and reorganise their sites, so that the chances of a distant anchor still being in place in a few months' time is pretty slim.

# Links and anchors

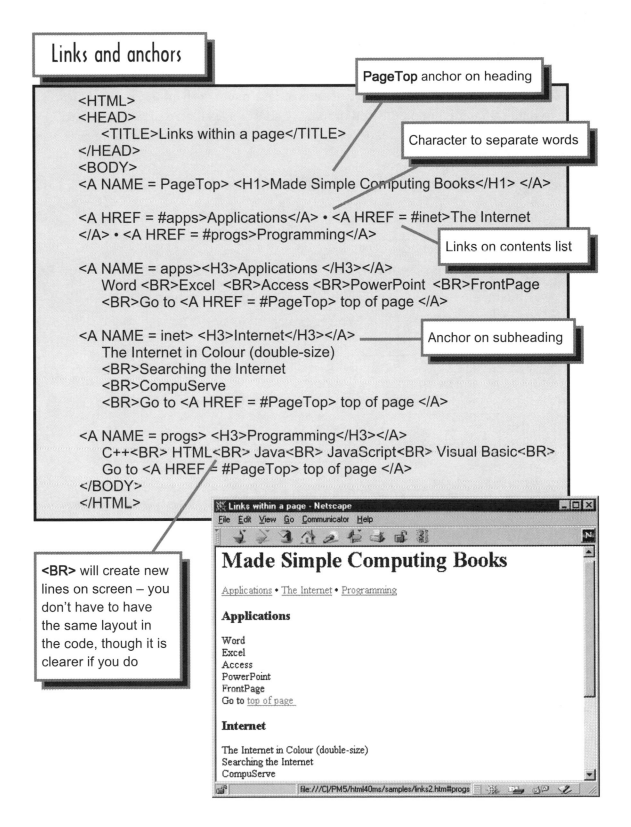

PageTop anchor on heading

```
<HTML>
<HEAD>
    <TITLE>Links within a page</TITLE>
</HEAD>
<BODY>
<A NAME = PageTop> <H1>Made Simple Computing Books</H1> </A>

<A HREF = #apps>Applications</A> • <A HREF = #inet>The Internet
</A> • <A HREF = #progs>Programming</A>

<A NAME = apps><H3>Applications </H3></A>
    Word <BR>Excel  <BR>Access <BR>PowerPoint  <BR>FrontPage
    <BR>Go to <A HREF = #PageTop> top of page </A>

<A NAME = inet> <H3>Internet</H3></A>
    The Internet in Colour (double-size)
    <BR>Searching the Internet
    <BR>CompuServe
    <BR>Go to <A HREF = #PageTop> top of page </A>

<A NAME = progs> <H3>Programming</H3></A>
    C++<BR> HTML<BR> Java<BR> JavaScript<BR> Visual Basic<BR>
    Go to <A HREF = #PageTop> top of page </A>
</BODY>
</HTML>
```

Character to separate words

Links on contents list

Anchor on subheading

**<BR>** will create new lines on screen – you don't have to have the same layout in the code, though it is clearer if you do

**Links within a page - Netscape**

File  Edit  View  Go  Communicator  Help

# Made Simple Computing Books

Applications • The Internet • Programming

**Applications**

Word
Excel
Access
PowerPoint
FrontPage
Go to top of page

**Internet**

The Internet in Colour (double-size)
Searching the Internet
CompuServe

file:///C|/PM5/html40ms/samples/links2.htm#progs

41

# Multi-page structures

Publishing your site as a set of interlinked pages will make it easier to maintain – it is simpler to add or remove short pages than to edit a long one – and quicker for your readers to find the material they want – as long as it is properly organised.

A personal home site might have this structure:

A business site may have a slightly more complex structure:

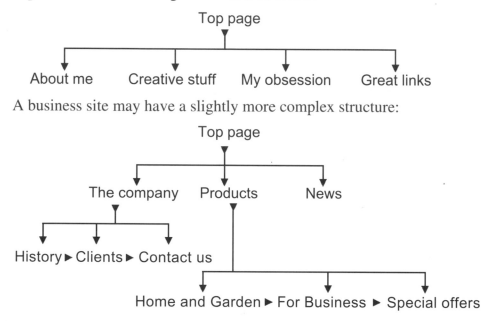

Entry to the top page is simple – when visitors give the URL of a site, that is where they will normally be taken. This is true for businesses (**www.bh.com**) and personal Web sites (**homepages.tcp.co.uk/~macbride**) – in both cases, the top page name (usually **index.html**) is assumed. They can only get deeper into the site if they know the names of the pages or if there are links from that top page. Where there are less than a dozen or so pages, links to them all can be listed in the top page; with a larger site, you need a hierarchy of pages, with links in the top page leading to 'top of area' pages, which hold the links to pages in their areas. What you must avoid is arranging pages solely in sequence. It can be useful to have links from one page to the next, but this mustn't be the only way to get to them.

# Paths to local files

The rules for addressing pages – and images, sounds or any other linked files – in your own site are the same when it is under development in your computer, and when it is published on the Web. You will not need to change any links – as long as you have the same structure of directories (or *folders*, as they are called in Windows).

It is by far the simplest to keep all of your files in the same directory – to link to a file, all that is then needed is the filename, e.g.

    <A HREF="freddy.htm">Meet my hamster</A>

If you have an awful lot of files, or several people are developing material for the site, you may be better with organised storage. Aim for a flat structure, with just one level of subdirectories, so that you keep the path simple.

A possible directory structure for a personal site – when uploading to your Web space at your service providers, create subdirectories with the same names and copy the corresponding files into each.

- To link from a page in the parent directory to one in a subdirectory, give the name of the subdirectory, a forward slash (/) and the filename, e.g.

    <A HREF="products/widgets.htm">Widgets</A>

- To link from a page in a subdirectory, to one in the parent directory, write "../" before the filename, e.g.

    <A HREF="../contents.htm">Return to the top page</A>

- To link to a page in another subdirectory, the path must go up to the parent, then down to the subdirectory, e.g.

    <A HREF="../contacts.htm">Contact us</A>

# <BASE ...>

Paths are normally relative to the location of the page containing the links. If necessary, you can make them relative to the position of another page by specifying that in the **<BASE ...>** tag:

    <BASE HREF = "http://www.bh.com/madesimple/htmlbook.htm">

# Links between pages

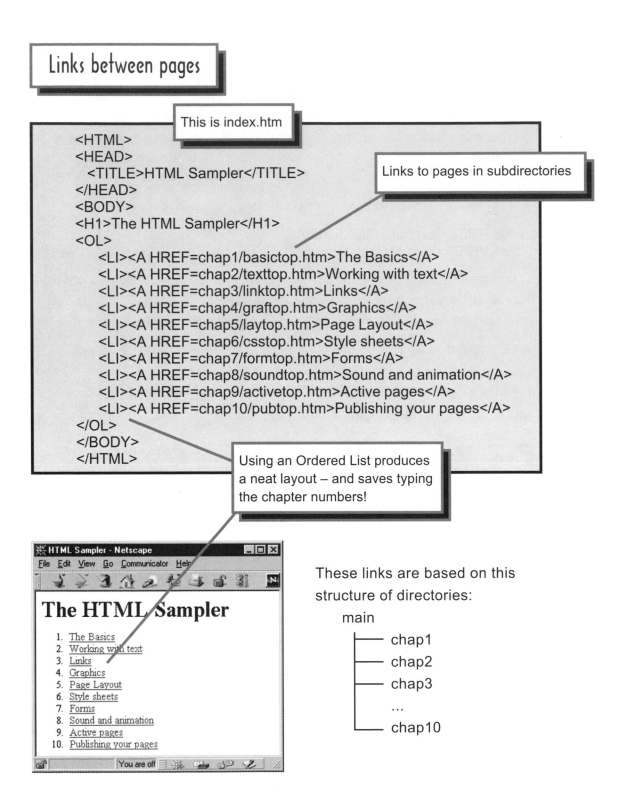

This is index.htm

```
<HTML>
<HEAD>
 <TITLE>HTML Sampler</TITLE>
</HEAD>
<BODY>
<H1>The HTML Sampler</H1>
<OL>
    <LI><A HREF=chap1/basictop.htm>The Basics</A>
    <LI><A HREF=chap2/texttop.htm>Working with text</A>
    <LI><A HREF=chap3/linktop.htm>Links</A>
    <LI><A HREF=chap4/graftop.htm>Graphics</A>
    <LI><A HREF=chap5/laytop.htm>Page Layout</A>
    <LI><A HREF=chap6/csstop.htm>Style sheets</A>
    <LI><A HREF=chap7/formtop.htm>Forms</A>
    <LI><A HREF=chap8/soundtop.htm>Sound and animation</A>
    <LI><A HREF=chap9/activetop.htm>Active pages</A>
    <LI><A HREF=chap10/pubtop.htm>Publishing your pages</A>
</OL>
</BODY>
</HTML>
```

Links to pages in subdirectories

Using an Ordered List produces a neat layout – and saves typing the chapter numbers!

**The HTML Sampler**

1. The Basics
2. Working with text
3. Links
4. Graphics
5. Page Layout
6. Style sheets
7. Forms
8. Sound and animation
9. Active pages
10. Publishing your pages

These links are based on this structure of directories:

```
main
├── chap1
├── chap2
├── chap3
│   ...
└── chap10
```

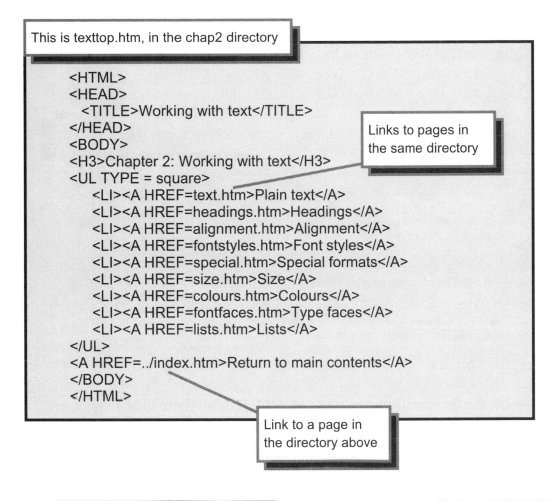

This is texttop.htm, in the chap2 directory

```
<HTML>
<HEAD>
  <TITLE>Working with text</TITLE>
</HEAD>
<BODY>
<H3>Chapter 2: Working with text</H3>
<UL TYPE = square>
   <LI><A HREF=text.htm>Plain text</A>
   <LI><A HREF=headings.htm>Headings</A>
   <LI><A HREF=alignment.htm>Alignment</A>
   <LI><A HREF=fontstyles.htm>Font styles</A>
   <LI><A HREF=special.htm>Special formats</A>
   <LI><A HREF=size.htm>Size</A>
   <LI><A HREF=colours.htm>Colours</A>
   <LI><A HREF=fontfaces.htm>Type faces</A>
   <LI><A HREF=lists.htm>Lists</A>
</UL>
<A HREF=../index.htm>Return to main contents</A>
</BODY>
</HTML>
```

Links to pages in the same directory

Link to a page in the directory above

The top page (opposite) and a top of section page (above) for the sample files in this book – at an early stage of development!

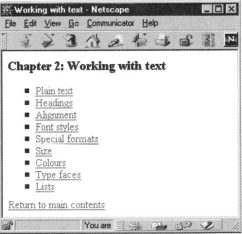

# Mailto: me

Links to other Web pages are by no means the only type of links. We'll look at some more in the last few pages of this chapter. Let's start with one of the simplest, but most important – **mailto**:. This takes an e-mail address as its URL, and when a visitor clicks on the link, it will start up their e-mail program, writing the linked address into the Recipient box.

On a personal Web site, a mailto: link gives your visitors an easy way to contact you.

```
<A HREF = mailto:fred.bloggs@inet.co.uk> Send me an e-mail </A>
```

On a commercial site, you could set up mailto: links to different departments within the organisation.

```
<A HREF = mailto:sales@widgets.co.uk> Sales enquiries </A>

<A HREF = mailto:jobs@widgets.co.uk> Job opportunities</A>

<A HREF = mailto:ignore@widgets.co.uk> Complaints</A>
```

## Feedback forms

mailto: links can also be used to get feedback from forms. The line:

```
<FORM ACTION =mailto:info@widgets.co.uk METHOD = Post>
```

sets up a form so that when the Submit button is clicked, the data entered by the user will be e-mailed to info@widgets.co.uk. This is not a fully reliable way to get feedback – it does not work if the form is being browsed by Internet Explorer – but we will return to this, and to an alternative way to get feedback on page 162.

---

 Take note

While you can put any e-mail address in a mailto: link, you will get into a lot of bother if you create e-mail links to people without their knowledge and approval. mailto: should normally only point to yourself, or to other people within your organisation – with their agreement!

# Other links

## Files

The **file://** link is used for sound, video, or any other type of data file. Where the link is within your own site, it can be omitted – in fact, it is far simpler to do so. Both of these lines link to the same sound file:

<A HREF = file:///C|/homepage/pets/woof.wav>Fido says Hi</A>

<A HREF = woof.wav>again</A>

Apart from the fact that **file:** references are a pain to write – notice the triple /// after file: and the vertical bar |, rather than a colon after C – they will need changing when you upload the files to the Web, as the files will then be on your access provider's server and will have a completely different path.

## FTP

FTP – File Transfer Protocol – is the standard method of copying files across the Internet. Browsers can download files using FTP, though if you want to make files available for others to download from your site, you will need special FTP server software. However, you can set up links to files stored in other (public) FTP sites. Use the **ftp://** link for this:

<A HREF = ftp://ftp.sunet.se/pub/pc/windows/games/yahtzee.zip >
Fancy a game of Yahtzee? </A>

## Newsgroups

To link to a newsgroup, use the **news:** link – note that, like **mailto:** this does not have forward slashes before the URL:

<A HREF = news:rec.humor.funny>Have a laugh</A>

## Gopher

The Gopher system was an early attempt to make it easier to navigate the Internet. Though it has now been long overtaken by the World Wide Web, there are still some useful resources – mainly academic – to be found within it. Follow up this **gopher://** link if you want to know more.

<A HREF = gopher://gopher.micro.umn.edu/>The original Gopher home at the University of Minnesota</A>

# Summary

❑     The World Wide Web is held together by HREF hypertext links between pages. A link can be to the home page of a site, to a page within in, or to a named point within a page.

❑     To have links within a page, you must set up named anchors which act as targets for HREF links.

❑     Long pages are slow to load and can be heavy going to read. A set of smaller, linked pages is a far more visitor-friendly alternative.

❑     When creating multi-page structures – or any site which uses many files – you may find files easier to manage if they are stored in a set of subfolders. If you do this, you must include the path to subfolder – or back up to the main folder, as appropriate – along with the filename when making links.

❑     The mailto: link offers a simple way to enable others to contact you by e-mail.

❑     HTML can also handle other types of links, the key ones being file://, ftp:// and news:

# 4 Graphics

Using graphics on your site ....... 50

Creating images ............... 52

GIFs .................... 55

JPEGs ................... 57

Background images ........... 58

Positioning and alignment ....... 60

Size .................... 62

Borders and spacing ........... 64

Links ................... 65

Image maps ................. 66

Summary .................. 70

# Using graphics on your site

Ah yes – pretty pictures and flashy animations, pulsating luminous buttons, big bubbly cartoon lettering, a whole gallery of those embarrassing birthday photos that you have of your friend… STOP!!! HOLD IT RIGHT THERE!!! I know there's a strong temptation to festoon your site with images like baubles on a Christmas tree, and it may all seem to work fine as you sit at home building and testing your site from your computer. But spare a thought for your audience, who will be accessing your masterpiece via a crowded phone line!

One of the trickiest bits of Web design is to strike a balance between attention-grabbing content and acceptable download times (and this goes double for sound and video clips). As you'll probably have discovered yourself when surfing the Net, it's frustrating to sit around waiting for some picture to come in, so the golden rule is always: *Small is beautiful.*

## Graphics formats

Web browsers can handle graphics is two formats: GIF and JPEG. These store the information in an image in different ways. Both formats use some method of compression to achieve the same goal, which is a high-quality image with a small file size. However, the differences between them mean that some images are more suited to the GIF format and others are smaller as JPEGs. Broadly speaking, cartoons, text or images with sharp lines of contrast and areas of flat colour should be GIFs; photos and images with smooth colour transitions should be JPEGs. You'll find a little more file format theory under the *Creating images* heading (page 52), but if you already have pictures and just want to get something up on your page, skip ahead for the moment to *Positioning and alignment* (page 60).

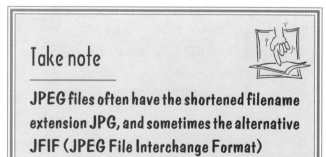

Take note

JPEG files often have the shortened filename extension JPG, and sometimes the alternative JFIF (JPEG File Interchange Format)

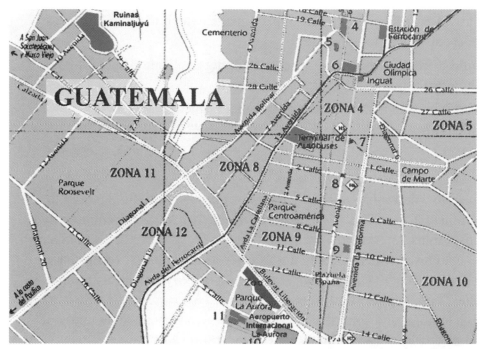

**Above**: Guatemala City street map –
47.9Kb as a GIF (used here) and 137Kb
as a JPEG. With simple block colours,
you will get the best compression in the
GIF format, without losing any clarity.

**Right**: Mother and child – 113Kb as a GIF
and 29.9Kb as a JPEG (used here). With
photographs and fine art, JPEGs are more
compact, yet retain the subtle toning
effects that are lost in a GIF.

# Creating images

There are three basic ways of creating an image, which in order of hardest (but most satisfying) to easiest are:

- build it from scratch using an image editing application such as Paint Shop Pro, Microsoft Image Composer, etc.
- scan it in from a photo, drawing or other printed image.
- nick it off the Web.

## Off the Web

Most people won't mind you using images from their site if it's purely for non-commercial home use – though in the interest of good community relations, I think you should e-mail them first to check. There are a number of image archives which friendly artists offer to home users: for instance, have a look at *Shawn's ClipArt and Webateria* at **http://www.inforamp.net/~dredge/**. You will also find huge collections of Web-ready art which are available to home and commercial users: there's a a very good directory of useful links at **http://www.thefreesite.com/graphics.htm**.

When you find an image you like, right-click on it, choose **Save picture as…**, and save it to file. You may need to give it a new, more recognisable, name – the original names are not always very meaningful.

| Open Link |
| Open Link in New Window |
| Save Target As… |
| Print Target |
| Show Picture |
| Save Picture As… |
| Set as Wallpaper |
| Copy |
| Copy Shortcut |
| Add to Favorites… |
| Properties |

---

### Tip

Be careful when using images from litigation-happy corporations! Monsanto probably wouldn't take too kindly to you borrowing their logo to use as a link to your Death By Genetic Mutation Homepage.

# Scanning

You'll need a scanner for this, and if you have one, you probably don't need me to tell you how to use it. Just remember to shrink the image down to a useable size before saving it, and use an appropriate file format – see GIFs and JPEGs on pages 55 – 57.

# From scratch

The image editing applications available as shareware are very sophisticated these days, and there's no point pretending I can teach you how to use any one of them in two pages. The ever-popular Paint Shop Pro, currently on version 5, is available to download from **http://www.jasc.com**, and if you're really serious, you can even order a copy of the official Paint Shop Pro tutorial book from the jasc website. Personally, I like to learn how to use this sort of thing by trial and error, because I have a lot of fun experimenting with all the tools and effects. You can always resort to the Help files – they're usually fairly impenetrable, but a bit of patience and a lot of switching between Help and a sample image will get you a long way. To get you started, here's a brief overview of some Paint Shop Pro 5's special features:

- **Picture Tubes** – these are like rubber stamps which produce random pictures from a themed selection. 'Coins', for example, is one of the sample tubes which comes with the package. When you use it, a picture of one of several different coins is dropped into the image where you clicked, complete with rather nice shadow. Different tubes work in different ways; with the 'Pointing Hands' tube, you need to click and hold the mouse button and then drag in the direction in which you want the hand to point. Further tubes are available from jasc, quite often on a seasonal theme. Play around, and see what you can do with them!

- **Layers** – instead of creating an image on a single canvas, you can work on several transparent layers, which can be manipulated independently of the others. You might have a background layer which is a photo of a mountain range, a second layer which is a cartoon of a plane, and a third layer which is some lettering. Now you can apply an airbrushing of snow over the mountains, move the plane around and change the size or colour of the lettering without affecting any of the other elements. Each time you want a new element on a separate layer, choose **New...** from the **Layers** menu, give it a name and start drawing. To toggle between layers, use the **Layers** palette. This is a powerful feature which gives you a lot of control over your picture, but DO keep a close eye on which layer you're working on at any time!

- The **Deformation** tool selects everything on one layer and allows you to move, rotate and reshape it. This is when you'll realise that you've drawn something on a layer you didn't mean to… but don't worry! Pick the **Freehand** select tool, draw around the bit you want to use on a new layer, and select **Promote to layer** from the **Selections** menu.

- The **Retouch** tool gives you a wide range of effects, from blurring (**Soften**) and smudging (**Push**) to colour enhancements (**Lightness**, **Hue**, **Saturation**, **Color** controls) and special effects (**Emboss**, **Dodge**).

Some of the effects that you can produce with Paint Shop Pro: all of the images here are from tubes, and the hand, dice and coins are in different layers, allowing the Retouch tool to be used on one without affecting another – notice how the blocks are softened, but the coins underneath stay crisp and clear.

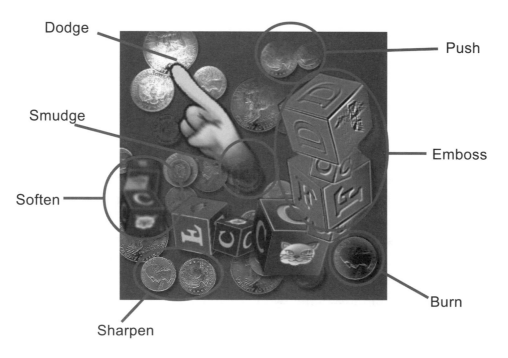

Dodge

Push

Smudge

Emboss

Soften

Burn

Sharpen

# GIFs

GIF stands for Graphics Interchange Format and was developed by the service providers Compuserve specifically for use on the Web. GIFs keep their file sizes small by limiting the number of colours used within an image so that each colour has only a short code to identify it – if you have 16 million colours, every colour must be assigned a unique code which distinguishes it from each of the other 15,999,999! You can set the colour depth of a GIF to 2 colours, 4, 8, 16, 32, 64, 128 or 256, depending on how many your image uses (many image-editing packages just give you 2, 16 or 256-colour options, but this is usually enough).

Using Paint Shop Pro, you must decrease the colour depth from the Colors menu before saving your image.

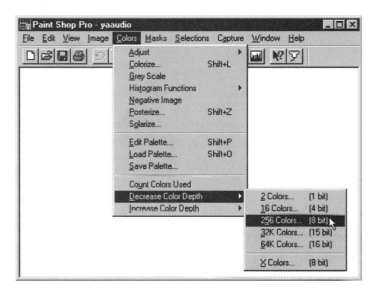

The GIF format also keeps files small by identifying repeated patterns in the image and labelling these; a zebra crossing, for example, has two basic patterns: a black stripe and a white stripe. Each of these patterns only needs to be defined once, then after the first two stripes, all subsequent stripes are identified with very short pieces of code which essentially just say 'black stripe' or 'white stripe'.

Other useful features of GIFs are transparent colours and interlacing. You can set one colour on a GIF to be 'transparent' and allow the background colour of the page to show through. This means that GIF images don't have to appear in a rectangle, but can appear as cut-outs.

An interlaced GIF, instead of sending the image to the browser line by line, sends one in every eight lines of pixels first, which are displayed either as a blocky, low-resolution image, or a sort of 'venetian blind' view. Then the next line below each of these is sent, giving a slightly clearer picture, then the next, and so on until the image is complete. This means that your viewers will get a rough idea of what they're looking at very quickly and won't have to sit there twiddling their thumbs and cursing you while they wait ...

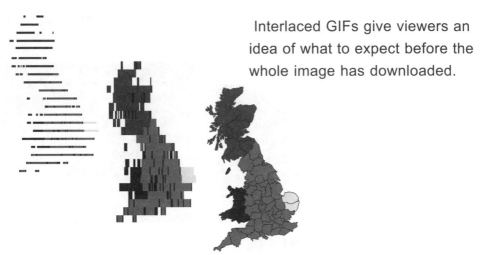

Interlaced GIFs give viewers an idea of what to expect before the whole image has downloaded.

## Take note

I don't want to get into anything beyond a brief outline of how the different file formats work here, because you probably don't need to know. However, if you're going to be using a lot of graphics on your site, then it's well worth spending half an hour at http://www.servtech.com/~dougg/graphics/index.html, where you'll find a full explanation of GIFs and JPEGs with some nice clear examples to show how the theory works in practice.

# JPEGs

JPEG stand for Joint Photographic Experts Group, and was developed – yup, you guessed it – by a group of photographic experts! They employed a very sophisticated system of mathematical functions which mimic our visual perception. Apparently. I'll be the first to admit that I haven't a clue how it really works, but the basic thing to appreciate is that JPEGs don't look at an image in terms of individual pixels, instead they map colour gradients across small blocks. This makes them sensitive to smooth colour changes, but not so hot when it comes to sharp geometric detail.

When you save an image as a JPEG, you can choose to set its compression level; high compression levels shrink files significantly, but the quality degrades with it. Fortunately JPEGs withstand a lot of compression before there is any noticeable loss of quality. Unfortunately, different image editors handle the compression levels differently, so there are no universal rules of thumb. In Paint Shop Pro, you can set a compression level of 1–99, 1 being the least compression and 99 the most; here's how the file size and quality change for a particular image:

| Compression level | File size | Loss of quality? |
|---|---|---|
| 1 | 287.0Kb | – |
| 20 | 91.8Kb | not noticeable |
| 40 | 78.6Kb | not noticeable |
| 60 | 35.9Kb | hmmm, nothing drastic |
| 80 | 22.8Kb | skin tones suffering |
| 99 | 10.0Kb | OK, it's a bit of a Picasso now |

JPEGs can be saved in standard or progressive encoding, which have a similar effect to non-interlaced and interlaced GIFs. However, whereas interlaced GIFs tend to be a fair bit larger than their non-interlaced equivalents, there's not a lot of difference between the two JPEG encodings.

# Background images

You've already learned how to change the background colour of your pages; if you want to be a bit more ambitious than that, you can set an image as a background instead. There are two basic types of image to consider here. Either way, you need one simple piece of code in the **\<BODY\>** tag:

```
<BODY BACKGROUND=image_name>
```

## Whole page images

One large image which covers the whole page. If you're opting for this, make sure that the image is fairly smooth and flat, and keep all the colours either light or dark – if you have areas of high contrast in the image, it'll be impossible to read any text over it. The exception to this rule is when you have a very carefully laid out page and you can guarantee that your text will end up overlying a clean area of the image.

If you have an image which you'd like to use, but it has too much contrast to use as it is, open up the image in Paint Shop Pro and adjust it. Either:

- fiddle with the colour controls – **Brightness**, **Lightness**, and **Contrast** will be particularly useful;

- or create a new layer over the image, set its **Opacity** to about 80–90% and fill it with the colour of your choice. Now you can fine tune the opacity using the slider on the **Layers** toolbar, or re-fill the layer with a different colour.

## Tiled images

If an image is smaller than the browser's window, it will be tiled across and down the page – you might try embossing your logo or some other picture and then ghosting it a little. Tiles can also be used to build up a larger pattern. Square blocks can be used to good effect – a veined tile for a marbled look, perhaps; or a black background with a few white dots for a deep-space background. Alternatively you can create long thin images which give you a patterned margin on the top or left margins of the screen.

In either case, you will have to be careful about designing the image so that the pattern at its edges match up properly – the top with the bottom, and the left with the right – if you want a smooth seamless effect.

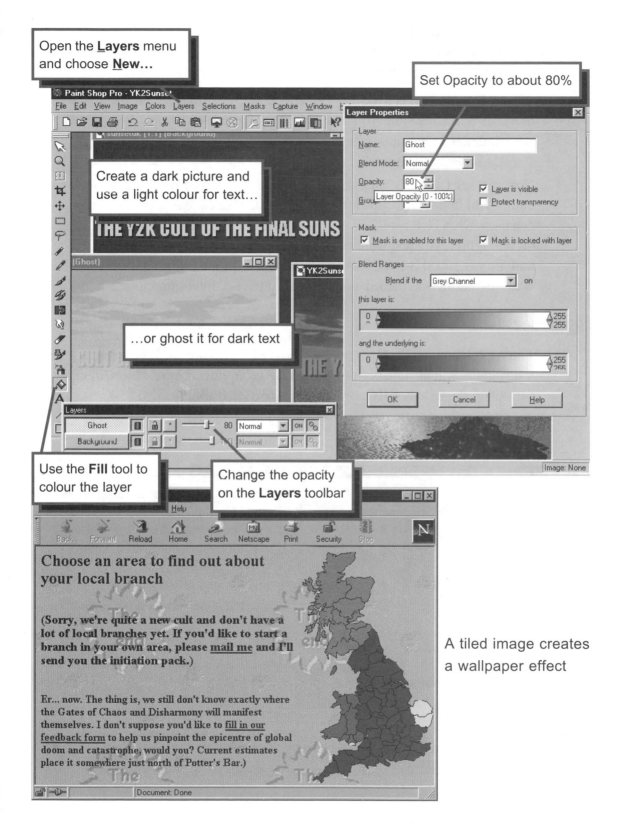

Open the **Layers** menu and choose **New…**

Set Opacity to about 80%

Create a dark picture and use a light colour for text…

…or ghost it for dark text

Use the **Fill** tool to colour the layer

Change the opacity on the **Layers** toolbar

A tiled image creates a wallpaper effect

**Paint Shop Pro - YK2Sunset**

File Edit View Image Colors Layers Selections Masks Capture Window

**Layer Properties**

Layer

Name: Ghost

Blend Mode: Normal

Opacity: 80

Layer Opacity (0 - 100%)

Group:

☑ Layer is visible
☐ Protect transparency

Mask

☑ Mask is enabled for this layer
☑ Mask is locked with layer

Blend Ranges

Blend if the Grey Channel on

this layer is:

0 — 255 / 255

and the underlying is:

0 — 255 / 255

OK    Cancel    Help

THE Y2K CULT OF THE FINAL SUNS

(Ghost)

YK2Sunse

Layers

Ghost    80 Normal ON

Background    Normal ON

Image: None

Help

Back  Forward  Reload  Home  Search  Netscape  Print  Security  Stop    N

**Choose an area to find out about your local branch**

(Sorry, we're quite a new cult and don't have a lot of local branches yet. If you'd like to start a branch in your own area, please mail me and I'll send you the initiation pack.)

Er… now. The thing is, we still don't know exactly where the Gates of Chaos and Disharmony will manifest themselves. I don't suppose you'd like to fill in our feedback form to help us pinpoint the epicentre of global doom and catastrophe, would you? Current estimates place it somewhere just north of Potter's Bar.)

Document: Done

# Positioning and alignment

The basic tag is **<IMG SRC…>**, which specifies the image source file. If the image is not in the same folder as the page, remember to specify a path:

<IMG SRC=filename.gif>

<IMG SRC=/images/pic.jpg>

You can set an image's position, size, and how text flows around it. By default, an image will appear on the left, as text does, but, as with text, you can use **<CENTER>** and **<P ALIGN=right>** to position it in the middle or on the right. If you just want a caption above or below, type a **<BR>** before and after the **<IMG SRC…>** and the image will get a line to itself. If you want text alongside the image, then you must set an alignment attribute.

## Aligning images with text

The **ALIGN** option is set within the **<IMG SRC…>** tag and takes the values top, middle, bottom, left, or right (the default is bottom). Any text immediately following the **<IMG SRC…>** tag is aligned accordingly.

<IMG SRC=Y2Ksunset.jpg ALIGN=top>

aligns the line of text in which the image appears with the top of the image.

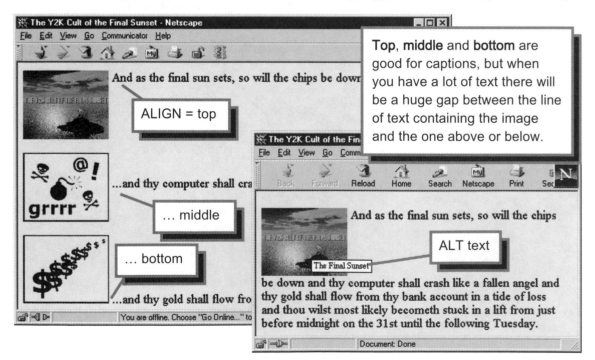

60

If you have a whole paragraph which you want to set alongside an image, use **ALIGN=left** or **right**. Left sets the image to the left of all text following the **<IMG SRC...>** tag, (and right to the right). It can be quite nice to break up a text-heavy page with an image or two interspersed with the words, but be warned: people visiting your site may use different sized browser windows, so don't try to arrange things so that you have a caption sitting neatly beneath an image. If you want a caption, incorporate it into the image and leave the text to flow where it will.

## Take note

*Everything* after the ‹IMG› tag is affected by the **ALIGN** option, including other images. To arrange images and blocks of text accurately, use tables (page 88) or style sheets (Chapter 6).

## ALTernative text

The **<IMG>** tag can take an **ALT=...** option which sets the text to appear if the page is viewed with image-loading turned off. With newer browsers, the same text will appear as a pop-up label if the user pauses the cursor over the image. The text must be enclosed in quotes, unless it is a single word. Here's the line that creates the ALT text in the screenshot opposite:

<IMG SRC=YK2sunset.jpg ALT=The Final Sunset ALIGN=TEXTTOP>

# Size

Images are automatically displayed at their natural size, but you can change this by setting the **WIDTH** and/or **HEIGHT** like so:

```
<IMG SRC=image.gif WIDTH=100 HEIGHT=150>
```

More often than not you'll want images to appear at their natural size, because enlarged images will lose definition, and shrunken images are usually a waste of download time – there's no point loading in a huge 500Kb image and then shrinking it down to a thumbnail. However, if you are repeating an image already loaded on the page, it will be saved in the browser's cache, and you don't need to worry about its file size again.

In any case, it's good practice to specify the dimensions, because it lets the browser set the page layout quickly and clearly. When a browser reads an HTML file, it goes through the text code first before loading in any images – you'll have noticed when surfing yourself those little icons which appear before an image is loaded in. If it comes across **WIDTH** and **HEIGHT** tags, it will leave an appropriate space; if not, it will only leave enough space for the icon and then have to shuffle things around later.

The **WIDTH** and **HEIGHT** options can be set in per cent as well as pixels, which calculates the size of the image as a percentage of the height and width of the browser window in which it's being displayed. This is useful for things like big page titles which you might want to fill the whole screen width, no matter what size your viewers' windows.

```
<IMG SRC=banner.gif WIDTH=100%>
```

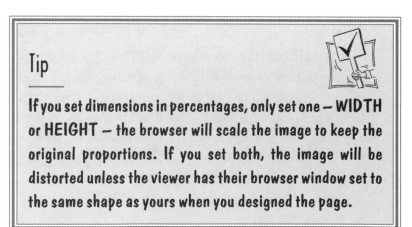

## Tip

If you set dimensions in percentages, only set one – **WIDTH** or **HEIGHT** – the browser will scale the image to keep the original proportions. If you set both, the image will be distorted unless the viewer has their browser window set to the same shape as yours when you designed the page.

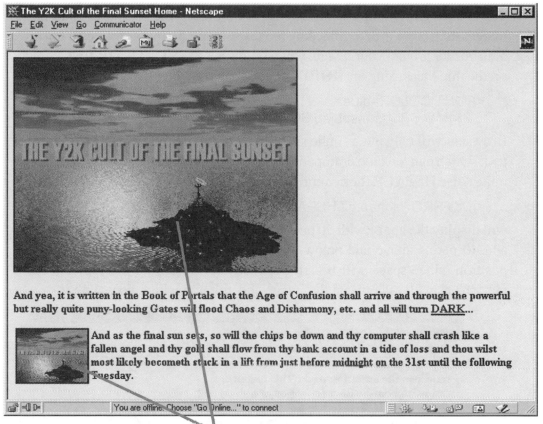

And yea, it is written in the Book of Portals that the Age of Confusion shall arrive and through the powerful but really quite puny-looking Gates will flood Chaos and Disharmony, etc. and all will turn <u>DARK</u>...

And as the final sun sets, so will the chips be down and thy computer shall crash like a fallen angel and thy gold shall flow from thy bank account in a tide of loss and thou wilst most likely becometh stuck in a lift from just before midnight on the 31st until the following Tuesday.

The same image is called up twice, but its size is set the second time; the page still loads quickly

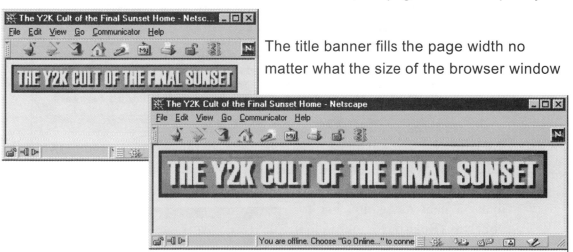

The title banner fills the page width no matter what the size of the browser window

# Borders and spacing

The **BORDER** option sets the thickness (in pixels) of a border around an image; the colour is determined by the text colour. So if you wanted a thick blue border around your image, you would set a **FONT COLOR** first, then set the thickness using the **BORDER** option within the **<IMG SRC...>** tag:

```
<FONT COLOR=blue>
    <IMG SRC=sunset.jpg BORDER=25>
```

Browsers will only put a single space between an image and any following text, which can look too cramped. To set a clear number of pixels around an image, use **HSPACE** (horizontal spacing) and **VSPACE** (vertical spacing).

```
<IMG SRC=ukmap.gif HSPACE=50 VSPACE=40>
```

will display the image with 50 pixels of clear space to the left and right of it, and 40 pixels above and below. Notice that this also affects the image's position, since space will be left between the image and the top or side margins as well as between the image and any text which goes with it.

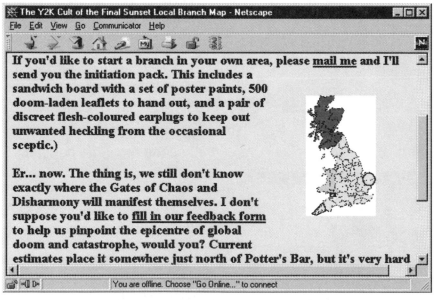

Sometimes it's useful to have *no* space between images; if you type **<IMG SRC...>** tags next to each other, the images will be displayed shoulder-to-shoulder. Several images next to each other, each with a different link, can make a neat navigation bar for your site. (Read on for more about links and navigation bars.)

# Links

An image can be used as a link in just the same way as a piece of text, and it's often more intuitive to click on a picture or a button to take you somewhere than on an underlined word. Just enclose the image in the anchor tags **<A HREF...>** and **</A>**:

```
<A HREF=ukmap.htm><IMG SRC=mapbuttn.gif></A>
```

The image is now a clickable link, and it is given a 2-pixel border in the **LINK** colour to show unsuspecting viewers that that's what it is. If you want to turn off the border, just set the **BORDER** option to 0.

## Navigation bars

A common way to help people find their way round your site is to build a navigation bar, which is a set of images or buttons linked to different pages. The simplest kind is a horizontal one across the top and/or bottom of a page; this is made from several **<A HREF...><IMG SRC...></A>** tags written consecutively:

```
<HTML>
<BODY>
<CENTER>
<A HREF=maln.htm><IMG SRC-home.gif BORDER = 0></A><A HREF =
ukmap.htm> <IMG SRC=map.gif BORDER = 0></A> <A HREF= form.htm>
<IMG SRC=fbackbut.gif BORDER = 0> </A> <A HREF= cash.htm> <IMG SRC
=givebut.gif BORDER = 0></A>
</CENTER>
</BODY>
</HTML>
```

HOME    UK MAP    FEEDBACK FORM    DONATIONS

Though you should generally keep lines of code short for the sake of clarity, there's no choice in this case: remember that a line break counts as a space in HTML, so you must put all the tags on one line with no spaces between them. You'll notice that I've used **<CENTER>** tags to drop the bar nicely into the middle of the screen. It's also worth setting the **BORDER** to 0 in each **<IMG SRC...>** tag so that your buttons join up seamlessly.

# Image maps

In an image map, different areas of a single image are set up as links to different places. By far the simplest way to deal with this is to use an HTML editor with an image map editing facility, because it can be very time-consuming. But it's always worth knowing how something works so that you can troubleshoot, so read on…

## The theory

First, you need to tell browsers to use your image as a map: give it a name inside the **<IMG SRC…>** tag with the **USEMAP** option. Note that you precede the name with a **#**:

```
<IMG SRC=ukmap.gif USEMAP="#ukmap">
```

The areas are defined in lines enclosed by **<MAP…> </MAP>** tags. Inside the first tag, you specify the name of the map you're referring to (you may have more than one on a page). Notice that the # is not written here:

```
<MAP NAME=ukmap>
```

Now you are ready to define a 'hotspot' (linked area) in an **<AREA…>** tag. There are four **SHAPE** options: **RECT** (rectangle), **CIRCLE**, **POLYGON** – which all need defining coordinates (**COORDS**) – and **DEFAULT**. The **<AREA…>** tag also needs an **HREF** to create the link:

```
<AREA SHAPE=… COORDS=… HREF=…>
```

The coordinates are pixel references: for instance, the middle of the top edge of a 55 by 55 pixel image is (27,0). If you're hand-coding the map, find yourself a pen and paper, and open your image in an image editing application such as Paint Shop Pro. Watch the status line as you move the mouse pointer over the map and note down the co-ordinates you need.

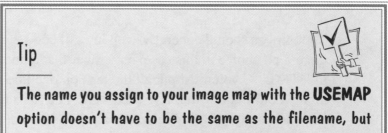

## Tip

The name you assign to your image map with the **USEMAP** option doesn't have to be the same as the filename, but there's no point complicating life unnecessarily.

# The practice

- For a **rectangle**, you only need to give the top left and lower right corner coordinates, which are given in the form "*x1,y1,x2,y2*".

- A **circle** needs just three numbers: the coordinates of its centre and the radius, given in pixels as "*x,y,radius*".

- The **polygon** option is where an image map editor really comes into its own, because it will take as many coordinates as you want to set, one for each vertex. In the example below, there are only four vertices, but I could have mapped out the shoreline of Cornwall much more closely.

- The **default** option sets a 'background' link for any part of the image not defined by any other shape.

Let's take a look at an example: I've superimposed the outlines of the linked shapes on the map so you can see what's what – you won't actually see anything in the browser's display.

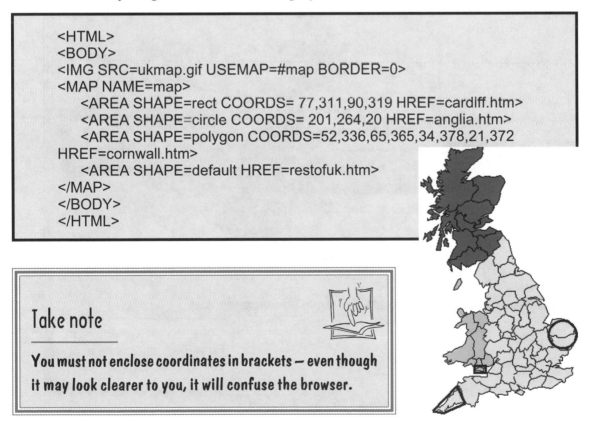

```
<HTML>
<BODY>
<IMG SRC=ukmap.gif USEMAP=#map BORDER=0>
<MAP NAME=map>
    <AREA SHAPE=rect COORDS= 77,311,90,319 HREF=cardiff.htm>
    <AREA SHAPE=circle COORDS= 201,264,20 HREF=anglia.htm>
    <AREA SHAPE=polygon COORDS=52,336,65,365,34,378,21,372
HREF=cornwall.htm>
    <AREA SHAPE=default HREF=restofuk.htm>
</MAP>
</BODY>
</HTML>
```

**Take note**

You must not enclose coordinates in brackets – even though it may look clearer to you, it will confuse the browser.

# Image maps using FrontPage

Microsoft FrontPage Express comes free with the latest versions of Internet Explorer, but unfortunately you can't use it to generate image maps; you need the full version of FrontPage for that.

Open up your page in FrontPage and click on the image you want to edit; there's a floating tool bar to select your shapes from, and then you just click away to your heart's content. Once a hotspot is defined, a dialogue box appears for you to set the link in. Now you can either just save the file, or choose **HTML...** from the **View** menu, and cut and paste the code into your HTML file. The former is easier, but has the unpleasant side-effect of adding all sorts of extra tags to your code. Cutting and pasting protects your file from this, but it can be tricky finding the code you want from amidst the rest of it!

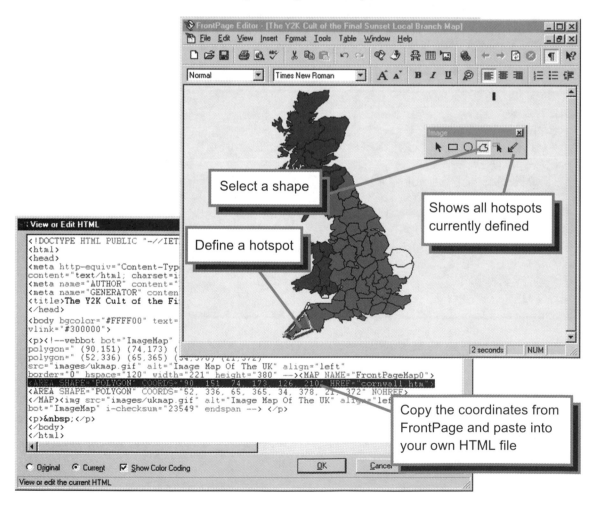

# Image maps using Map Edit

Map Edit is designed purely for creating and editing image maps, and won't change anything but the code inside the **<MAP...> </MAP>** tags. Open the page in Map Edit, and you will be asked to choose from a list of images on that page. Select one, click **OK**, and away you go. The toolbar holds the standard shapes, but has other tools for editing your hotspots. The dialogue box for defining the link also gives you the option to add a little JavaScript. We'll look closer at JavaScript later (page 151), but here's a snippet which puts a message in the browser's status line. In the **onMouseOver** box, type:

    self.status= 'your message appears here'; return=true

This tells the browser to write this message, rather than the normal URL, when your viewer moves the mouse pointer over the link. To remove the message when the mouse is moved off the link, use the **onMouseOut** box:

    self.status="; return=true

Note that those are two single quotes with nothing in between, not one double quote. You are actually telling the browser to overwrite the previous message with '(nothing)'.

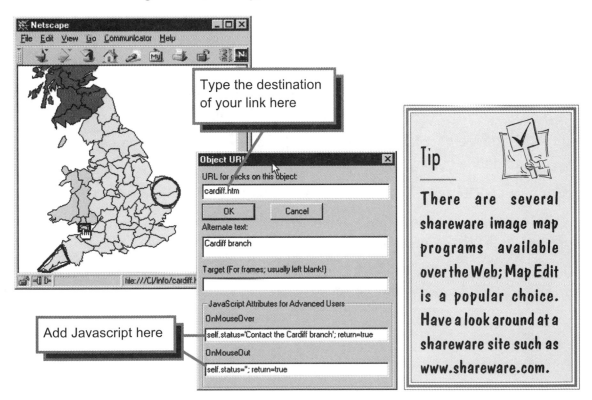

Type the destination of your link here

Add Javascript here

**Tip**

There are several shareware image map programs available over the Web; Map Edit is a popular choice. Have a look around at a shareware site such as www.shareware.com.

69

# Summary

- ❏ Graphics can enhance a page, but add significantly to its download time. Make sure that any images you use are worth the wait!

- ❏ The Web is a great source of images, or you can scan in your own or create them from scratch using a graphics application such as Paint Shop Pro.

- ❏ To be displayed on Web pages, graphics must be in one of two formats: GIFs are good for cartoons and other images that use a limited range of colours; JPEGs are best for photographs.

- ❏ If you want background images for your pages, you can either use one large graphic, or a small one that will tile to fill the window. In either case they should be coloured carefully to allow a good contrast with the page's text.

- ❏ The <IMG> tag and standard alignment options give limited control over the positioning of images and related text.

- ❏ The displayed size of images can be controlled by setting the WIDTH and HEIGHT options.

- ❏ A border can be set round an image. If the image carries a link, it will normally have a 2 pixel border – set it to 0 if a border is not wanted.

- ❏ Setting a vertical and/or horizontal space around an image can help to define the layout of images and text.

- ❏ An HREF link can be applied to an image in the same way as to text.

- ❏ By using a graphic as an image map, it can be made to carry many different hypertext links.

# 5 Page layout

Layout methods . . . . . . . . . . . . . . . . .72

Simple tables . . . . . . . . . . . . . . . . .74

Formatting tables . . . . . . . . . . . . . .76

Cell size . . . . . . . . . . . . . . . . . . .80

Advanced tables . . . . . . . . . . . . . . .82

Borders and rules . . . . . . . . . . . . . .86

Tables for page layout . . . . . . . . . . .88

Frames . . . . . . . . . . . . . . . . . . . .92

Filling in the frames . . . . . . . . . . . .94

Links and targets . . . . . . . . . . . . . .95

Changing a frame's look . . . . . . . . .97

Summary . . . . . . . . . . . . . . . . . . .98

# Layout methods

The most accurate way to control the layout of your pages is to use style sheets – provided you have a browser which supports HTML 4.0, and you want to cater solely for those of your viewers who also have such browsers. This is not quite as elitist as it sounds, but you may nevertheless prefer your pages to be accessible by pretty much everyone, in which case you'll need to plan your page layout using tables and frames instead.

## Tables

As well as simply a means of organising data, tables can be given invisible borders and used in a hidden way to divide a page up into different areas. These areas can then hold images and text - or can be left blank, as spacers between other elements. We'll start off by looking at some straightforward data tables before moving on to using tables for page layout, so that you can get to grips with the mechanics of constructing tables first.

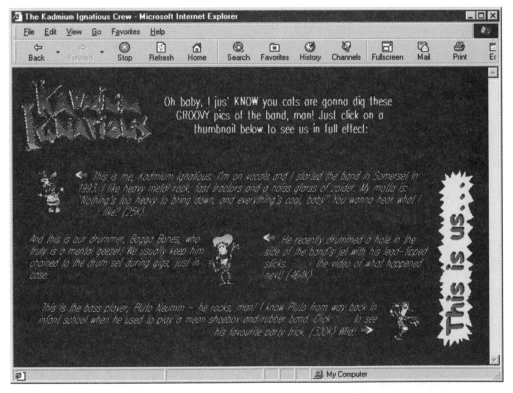

The page in the main frame above is laid out using tables.

# Frames

Frames are useful for keeping something permanently visible, such as a navigation bar or your company logo, while viewers scroll and browse through other pages. They divide the browser window up into areas, each of which holds a separate page. A small HTML document is created first which tells the browser how to divide up the window; separate HTML documents are then required to generate the content for each frame. Links from a frame can be set to display the new page in the same frame or in others, or they can replace the whole frameset.

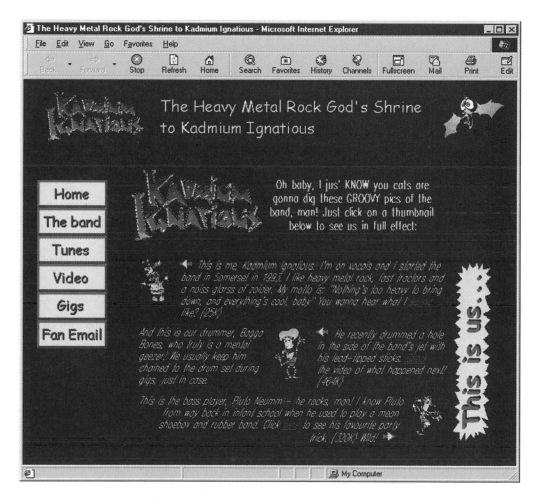

You can't see them, but this page uses frames and tables in its layout.

# Simple tables

We'll start with ordinary tables, the kind that hold rows and columns of data, so that you can see what's going on before we move on to discuss how they can be applied to page layout.

A table is made up of rows and columns which intersect to form *cells*. The code which creates a table begins with a **<TABLE...>** tag, and is then defined row by row with **<TR>** (table row) tags. The columns are then slotted in from left to right as the browser comes across cell tags (**<TD>** – table data), and the table is closed with a **</TABLE>** tag. A simple table could be coded like this:

```
<HTML>
<BODY>
    A simple table:
    <P>
    <TABLE>
        <TR>
            <TD>top left </TD>
            <TD>top right </TD>
        </TR>
        <TR>
            <TD>bottom left </TD>
            <TD>bottom right </TD>
        </TR>
    </TABLE>
</BODY>
</HTML>
```

To see more clearly what's going on, set a **BORDER** thickness inside the **<TABLE...>** tag: **<TABLE BORDER=2>**. This draws rules between cells and around the outside of the table. The outer borders are usually displayed by browsers with a 3-D effect – the top and left edges being a lighter colour than the bottom and right edges. Navigator does a fair job of picking a light and dark colour to match the page background; Explorer will use silver and dark grey unless you specify the highlight and lowlight with the options **BORDERCOLORLIGHT** and **BORDERCOLORDARK**.

If you want a caption for your table to explain what it is, use the **<CAPTION>** **</CAPTION>** tags. These align the text centrally above the table – or below it if you set the option **ALIGN=bottom** inside the first tag.

```
<HTML>
<BODY>
   A simple table:<BR>
   <TABLE>
      <TR>
         <TD>top left </TD>
         <TD>top right </TD>
      </TR>
      <TR>
         <TD>bottom left </TD>
         <TD>bottom right </TD>
      </TR>
   </TABLE>
   <P>
   <TABLE BORDER=2>
   <CAPTION ALIGN="bottom">And now with rules, plus a
      bottom-aligned caption</CAPTION>
      <TR>
         <TD>top left </TD>
         <TD>top right </TD>
      </TR>
      <TR>
         <TD>bottom left </TD>
         <TD>bottom right </TD>
      </TR>
   </TABLE>
</BODY>
</HTML>
```

Indenting the code helps to make it more readable by emphasising which **<TD>** lines make up each row of the table

Netscape

File  Edit  View  Go  Communicator  Help

A simple table:

top left      top right

bottom left  bottom right

| top left | top right |
| bottom left | bottom right |

And now with rules, plus
a bottom-aligned caption

You are offline. Choose "C

## Tip

As browsers piece a table together bit by bit, they can lay out the page faster if you state at the beginning how many columns there are — in the same way as you should specify the size of your images (see p. 60).

Type COLS= *number of columns* inside the <TABLE...> tag, e.g. <TABLE COLS=5>.

# Formatting tables

Besides having a border, there are other options which can be put in the <TABLE...> tag to determine its properties:

- **WIDTH** sets the width of the table in pixels, or as a percentage of the browser window. If you don't specify a width, a table is made just wide enough to hold its contents, or the width of the window for larger tables.

- **ALIGN** – tables which are less than the full window width can be aligned centrally or to the right of the page, as for text and images.

- **BGCOLOR** sets a background colour for the table if you want it to stand out from the rest of the page – if you don't set one, the page background is used.

- **BACKGROUND** as with page backgrounds, you can use an image as a table background instead of a flat colour.

- **CELLSPACING** sets the distance in pixels between each row and each column, providing a kind of 'frame' around the cells.

- **CELLPADDING** sets the distance in pixels between the contents of each cell and its borders.

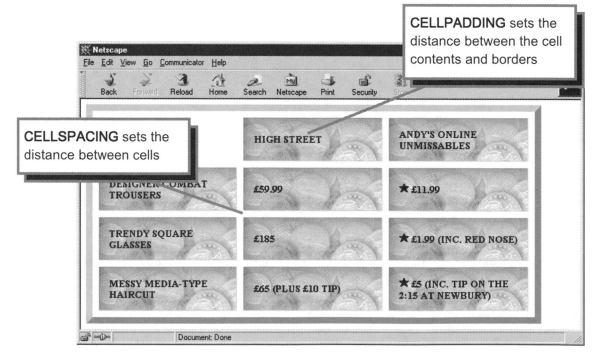

CELLPADDING sets the distance between the cell contents and borders

CELLSPACING sets the distance between cells

| | HIGH STREET | ANDY'S ONLINE UNMISSABLES |
|---|---|---|
| DESIGNER COMBAT TROUSERS | £59.99 | ★ £11.99 |
| TRENDY SQUARE GLASSES | £185 | ★ £1.99 (INC. RED NOSE) |
| MESSY MEDIA-TYPE HAIRCUT | £65 (PLUS £10 TIP) | ★ £5 (INC. TIP ON THE 2:15 AT NEWBURY) |

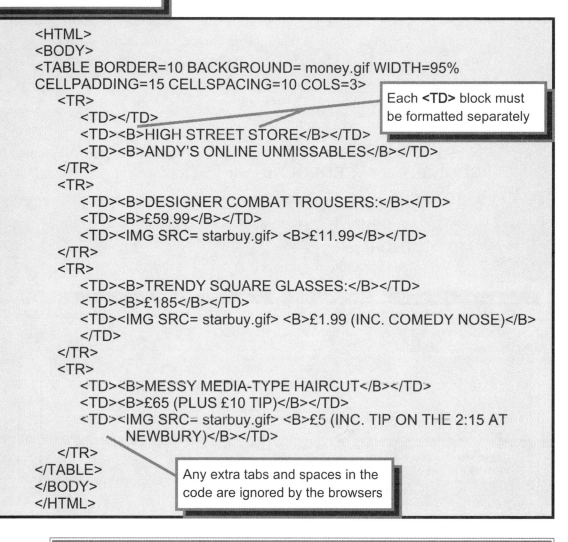

```
<HTML>
<BODY>
<TABLE BORDER=10 BACKGROUND= money.gif WIDTH=95%
CELLPADDING=15 CELLSPACING=10 COLS=3>
    <TR>
        <TD></TD>
        <TD><B>HIGH STREET STORE</B></TD>
        <TD><B>ANDY'S ONLINE UNMISSABLES</B></TD>
    </TR>
    <TR>
        <TD><B>DESIGNER COMBAT TROUSERS:</B></TD>
        <TD><B>£59.99</B></TD>
        <TD><IMG SRC= starbuy.gif> <B>£11.99</B></TD>
    </TR>
    <TR>
        <TD><B>TRENDY SQUARE GLASSES:</B></TD>
        <TD><B>£185</B></TD>
        <TD><IMG SRC= starbuy.gif> <B>£1.99 (INC. COMEDY NOSE)</B>
        </TD>
    </TR>
    <TR>
        <TD><B>MESSY MEDIA-TYPE HAIRCUT</B></TD>
        <TD><B>£65 (PLUS £10 TIP)</B></TD>
        <TD><IMG SRC= starbuy.gif> <B>£5 (INC. TIP ON THE 2:15 AT
            NEWBURY)</B></TD>
    </TR>
</TABLE>
</BODY>
</HTML>
```

Each **<TD>** block must be formatted separately

Any extra tabs and spaces in the code are ignored by the browsers

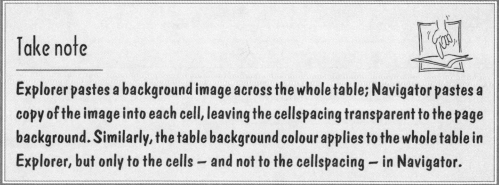

## Take note

**Explorer pastes a background image across the whole table; Navigator pastes a copy of the image into each cell, leaving the cellspacing transparent to the page background. Similarly, the table background colour applies to the whole table in Explorer, but only to the cells — and not to the cellspacing — in Navigator.**

# Formatting cells

By default, the contents of a cell are aligned horizontally to the left and vertically to the middle of each cell. This can be changed for each cell by setting options in its **<TD>** tag – **ALIGN** for horizontal alignment and **VALIGN** for vertical:

    <TD ALIGN= center VALIGN= bottom>

Sets this at the bottom of a cell, in the centre.

The background of a cell can also be changed to highlight it, using the same **BGCOLOR** and **BACKGROUND** options as for formatting the table:

    <TD BACKGROUND= money.gif><B>£185</B></TD>

This would overwrite any background image set at **TABLE** level.

    <TD BGCOLOR=yellow>

Sets a yellow background for this cell.

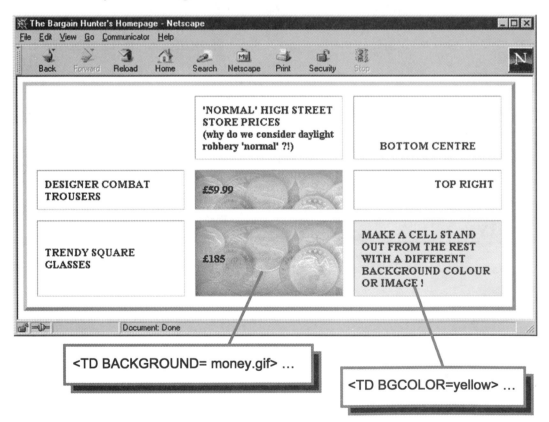

# Formatting text in tables

Text colour can't be set for a table as a whole – it follows the **TEXT COLOR** set in the **<BODY>** tag by default – and nor can text size, even if you add **<FONT COLOR... SIZE... ></FONT>** tags around the table code. However, the **<FONT FACE...>** tag does work – in Internet Explorer though not in Navigator – and will set a default type face for the text in a table. If you want to format text within cells, you have to use the **<FONT...>** tag inside each pair of **<TD></TD>** tags (these settings will override any default formatting). Unfortunately you'll have to do it separately for each cell, even if you want the same effect in every cell:

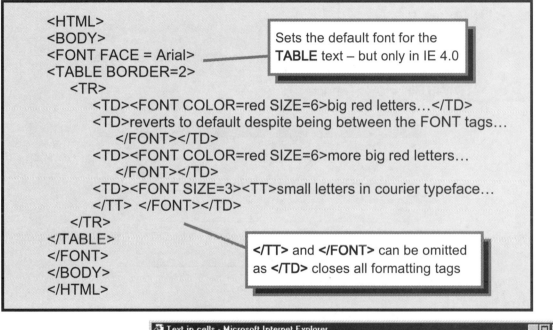

```
<HTML>
<BODY>
<FONT FACE = Arial>
<TABLE BORDER=2>
   <TR>
      <TD><FONT COLOR=red SIZE=6>big red letters...</TD>
      <TD>reverts to default despite being between the FONT tags...
         </FONT></TD>
      <TD><FONT COLOR=red SIZE=6>more big red letters...
         </FONT></TD>
      <TD><FONT SIZE=3><TT>small letters in courier typeface...
         </TT> </FONT></TD>
   </TR>
</TABLE>
</FONT>
</BODY>
</HTML>
```

Sets the default font for the **TABLE** text – but only in IE 4.0

**</TT>** and **</FONT>** can be omitted as **</TD>** closes all formatting tags

79

# Cell size

The size of a cell is determined mainly by what's in it, since it's got to be big enough to hold its contents, obviously. If you've specified the width of the whole table, then each column is given an equal width, all other things being equal. However, all other things aren't usually equal! Some attempt is made by most browsers to give more room to those cells with more in them than others, but with varying degrees of success.

If you want to make sure that your table is laid out the way it was intended, you should specify the widths of the cells. A cell's **WIDTH** can be set to a number of pixels, or as a percentage of the whole table width, inside each **<TD...>** tag:

```
<TD WIDTH=90%>
    This cell might hold a product description, followed by its...
</TD>
<TD WIDTH=10%>...price</TD>
```

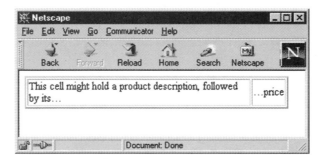

## But it doesn't work!

Unfortunately, not all browsers seem to handle this particular piece of code very well once you get beyond very basic tables, including Netscape Navigator, I'm afraid to say. The best way I've found to get around the problem is to patch your table together with some transparent images to act as spacers. When these images appear on the page, they will be completely invisible, but will force the columns into the size you want. It can be a slightly hit-and-miss affair, so let's take a closer look at how to use spacers in tables.

## Using spacers in tables

First of all, you will need to create an invisible image, and you would be wise to also create a nice lurid coloured version for test purposes. Fire up your image editing application and create a new image. It might as well be very small – when you tell the browser to enlarge it, you needn't worry about losing definition because it's going to be invisible! Pick a colour, and save the image as something like 'pink.gif', then set pink (or whatever vile colour you've chosen) to be the transparent colour, and save it again as your spacer.

Now add an extra row to the table, putting your lurid image in each cell and setting its **WIDTH** and **HEIGHT**. The **HEIGHT** should be small – 1 or 2 – so that it doesn't force a thick blank row before the rest of the table. The **WIDTH** is the important bit – work out roughly how wide each cell should be and test it in a browser. You'll be able to see from your coloured image where adjustments need to be made, and can then fine-tune the code. Once you're happy with the layout, replace the image with your invisible spacer.

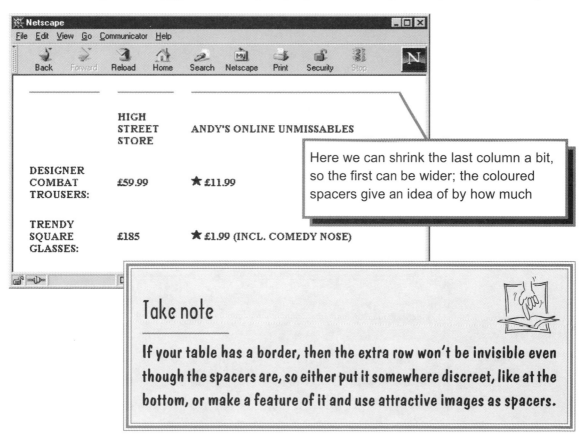

Here we can shrink the last column a bit, so the first can be wider; the coloured spacers give an idea of by how much

**Take note**

If your table has a border, then the extra row won't be invisible even though the spacers are, so either put it somewhere discreet, like at the bottom, or make a feature of it and use attractive images as spacers.

# Advanced tables

HTML 4.0 has a couple of features which make for smarter tables – the table can be divided into groups of rows and columns and formatting applied to all cells in a group, and there is greater control over how borders and rules between cells are displayed. It should be noted that only the newer browsers IE4.0 and higher, and Netscape 6.0, fully support these features. Let's have a quick look at the theory anyway.

## Groups of rows

Tables can be split into three sections – head, body and foot – and the cells in these can be formatted all at once. This is their value in table layout. In fact, the real idea behind the grouping is that future programs will be able to interpret tables correctly, converting information into a database format, for example, or printing out large tables, with headers and footers on each page.

The tags you need are:

● **<THEAD...>** for the group of rows which make up the table head

● **<TFOOT...>** for the foot

● **<TBODY...>** for the body

Each of these tags is then followed by **<TR>** and **<TD>** tags which define cells and their contents in the usual way. Notice that the head and foot groups come first, so that browsers can start to lay out the table without trawling through all the body rows – there could be hundreds! This is why the **<TFOOT>** and **<TBODY>** sections seem to be in the wrong order.

Inside the **<THEAD...>**, **<TFOOT...>**, and **<TBODY...>** tags you can set the alignment and background colour for the cells in each group in the same way as for any individual cell.

## Take note

A table can only have one head and one foot, but it can have several separately defined and formatted 'bodies' – just start a new group with a **<TBODY...>** tag and carry on adding rows.

```
<HTML>
<BODY>
<TABLE BORDER=1>
<THEAD BGCOLOR=orange ALIGN=center VALIGN=bottom>
    <TR>
        <TD>Title</TD>  <TD>Order<BR>code</TD>
    </TR>
<TFOOT BGCOLOR=red ALIGN=right>
    <TR>
        <TD COLSPAN=2>State CD, Vinyl or DVD on your order</TD>
    </TR>
<TBODY BGCOLOR=cyan>
    <TR>
        <TD>Ignatious rocks! ~ The original album</TD>
        <TD>KAD/001</TD>
    </TR>
<TBODY BGCOLOR=yellow>
    <TR>
        <TD>Kadmium IS heavy metal! ~ The gold-selling follow-up</TD>
        <TD>KAD/002</TD>
    </TR>
    <TR>
        <TD>Caesium the day! ~ The LP that went platinum</TD>
        <TD>KAD/0003</TD>
    </TR>
    <TR>
        <TD>Stop the PUNishment ~ Limited edition titanium disc with fur trim</TD>
        <TD>KAD/0004</TD>
    </TR>
</TABLE>
</BODY>
</HTML>
```

The table foot is defined before the table body

The main body of the table can be sub-divided into **<TBODY>** groups

Groups of rows - Microsoft Internet Explorer

File   Edit   View   Go   Favorites   Help

Back   Forward   Stop   Refresh   Home   Search   Favorites   History   Channels

| Title | Order code |
|---|---|
| Ignatious rocks! ~ The original album | KAD/001 |
| Kadmium IS heavy metal! ~ The gold-selling follow-up | KAD/002 |
| Caesium the day! ~ The LP that went platinum | KAD/0003 |
| Stop the PUNishment ~ Limited edition titanium disc with fur trim | KAD/0004 |
| State CD, Vinyl or DVD on your order | |

D                                    My Computer

83

## Groups of columns

Columns can also be grouped together and jointly formatted, using the **<COLGROUP...>** tag. The **<COLGROUP>** tag is placed immediately after the **<TABLE...>** tag, before any table data, to define column widths so that the browser knows how to set out the table from the beginning. As for rows, the tag can be used to set default cell alignment and background. Besides the formatting options, there are two which can be set for a group of columns:

● **SPAN** determines how many columns the group contains

● **WIDTH** sets the default width of each column in the group

The code below would set up a table with 6 columns; the first at 200 pixels wide, and the other 5 at 10% of the browser window each:

```
<TABLE>
   <COLGROUP WIDTH=200>
   <COLGROUP SPAN=5 WIDTH=10%>
   <THEAD>
      <TR>...
```

## Individual columns

Within a group of columns, you can format individual columns with the **<COL...>** tag. Why bother to put it into a group then? Well, as we shall see over the page, row and column groups can have borders drawn around them; you may want to enclose a group of columns in a border, but distinguish between individual columns with a change of background.

If a **<COLGROUP...>** is followed by any **<COL>** tags, the **SPAN** option is ignored and the **<COL>** tags counted instead. If you want to format just one column in a group, make sure you add empty **<COL>** tags before and after it so that you don't throw your other column formatting out of kilter.

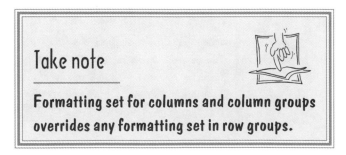

Take note

Formatting set for columns and column groups overrides any formatting set in row groups.

Sets default formats for the columns

```
...
<TABLE BORDER=5>
    <COLGROUP SPAN=2 ALIGN=left>
        <COL WIDTH=40% BGCOLOR=navy>
        <COL WIDTH=10% BGCOLOR=olive>
    <COLGROUP SPAN=3 WIDTH=50 ALIGN=center BGCOLOR= maroon>
        <COL>
        <COL BGCOLOR=blue>
        <COL>
<COLGROUP WIDTH=50 BGCOLOR=purple>
<THEAD VALIGN=top ALIGN=center BGCOLOR=red>
    <TR>
        <TD ROWSPAN=2 ALIGN=center>TITLE</TD>
        <TD ROWSPAN=2 ALIGN=center>ORDER CODE</TD>
        <TD COLSPAN=3>AVAILABLE ON:</TD>
        <TD ROWSPAN=2>PRICE</TD>
    </TR>
    <TR>
        <TD>CD</TD>  <TD>VINYL</TD>  <TD>DVD</TD>
    </TR>
<TFOOT>
    <TR>
        <TD COLSPAN=6 ALIGN=center BGCOLOR=red>~ Please specify which
        format when ordering ~ Thanks for supporting us ~ Enjoy the tunes ~ </TD>
    </TR>
<TBODY>
    <TR>
        <TD>Ignatious rocks! ~ The original album</TD>
...
```

Annotations:

- Resets the background for the middle column only in this group
- Overrides the default formats for the column
- There can be more than one row in the **THEAD** or **TFOOT**
- Spans two rows
- Spans three columns

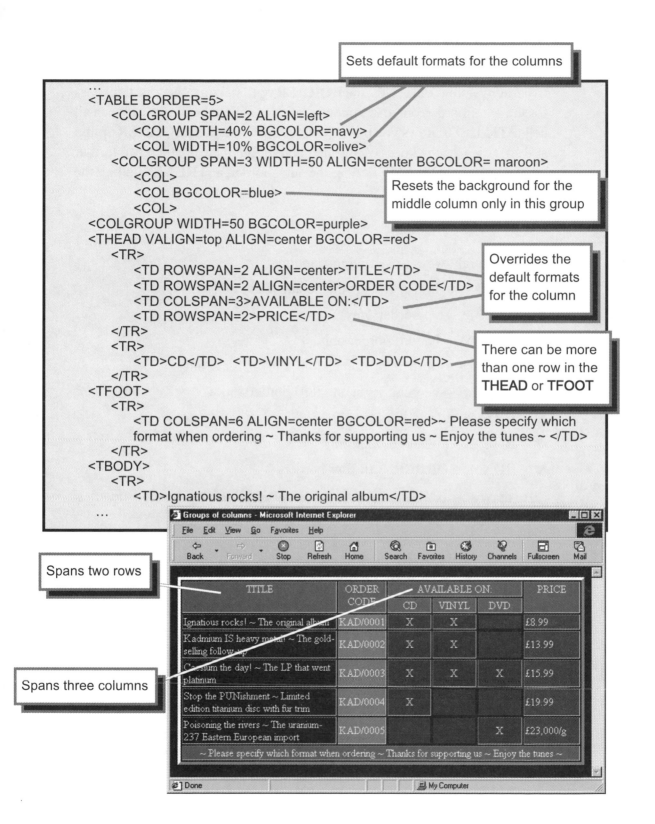

Browser window — Groups of columns - Microsoft Internet Explorer

| TITLE | ORDER CODE | AVAILABLE ON: | | | PRICE |
| --- | --- | --- | --- | --- | --- |
| | | CD | VINYL | DVD | |
| Ignatious rocks! ~ The original album | KAD/0001 | X | X | | £8.99 |
| Kadmium IS heavy metal! ~ The gold-selling follow-up | KAD/0002 | X | X | | £13.99 |
| Caesium the day! ~ The LP that went platinum | KAD/0003 | X | X | X | £15.99 |
| Stop the PUNishment ~ Limited edition titanium disc with fur trim | KAD/0004 | X | | | £19.99 |
| Poisoning the rivers ~ The uranium-237 Eastern European import | KAD/0005 | | | X | £23,000/g |
| ~ Please specify which format when ordering ~ Thanks for supporting us ~ Enjoy the tunes ~ | | | | | |

# Borders and rules

In earlier versions of HTML, the **BORDER** option for a table set a thickness for the outer border, but also implied that rules should be drawn between all cells. HTML 4.0 allows you more flexibility with this. The **BORDER** option still specifies the thickness of the outer border, but there are then two further options to define: **FRAME** defines the outer border, and **RULES** defines the rules between cells.

## Frame

There are eight ways of setting this option:

- **VOID** – no border (this is the default value)
- **ABOVE** – top border only
- **BELOW** – bottom border only
- **HSIDES** – Horizontal (top and bottom) borders only
- **VSIDES** – Vertical (right and left) borders only
- **LHS** – left-hand border only
- **RHS** – right-hand border only
- **BOX** or **BORDER** – all four borders

So to draw a 5-pixel border above and below the table but not round the sides:

```
<TABLE BORDER=5 FRAME=HSIDES>
```

## Rules

The five options for defining rules are:

- **NONE** – no rules
- **GROUPS** – rules between row groups and column groups only.
- **ROWS** – rules between rows only.
- **COLS** – rules between columns only.
- **ALL** – rules between all cells.

The default value is supposed to be **NONE**, but if you look carefully at the screenshot on the previous page, you should be able to see that cells which have content have rules, and those which don't, don't.

```
<HTML>
<HEAD>
<TITLE>Borders and rules</TITLE>
</HEAD>
<BODY BGCOLOR=black TEXT=white>
<TABLE BORDER=5 RULES=groups CELLSPACING=0>
<COLGROUP SPAN=2 ALIGN=left>
    <COL WIDTH=40% BGCOLOR=navy>
    <COL WIDTH=10% BGCOLOR=olive>
```

**CELLSPACING** set to 0 so that you can see more clearly where the rules are

Rules are drawn between groups of rows and groups of columns

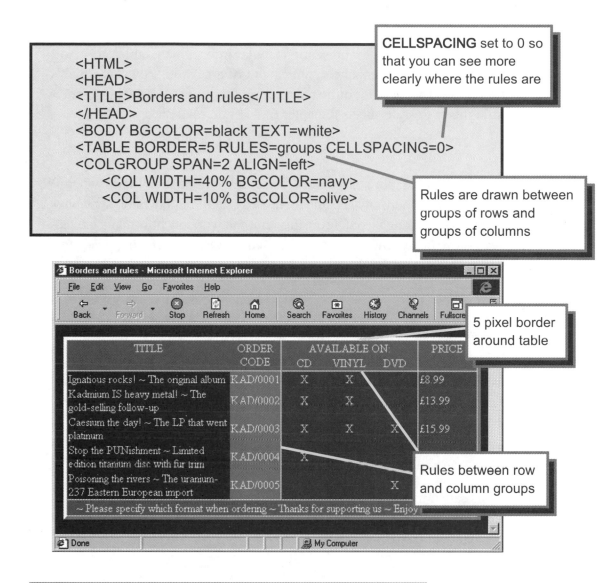

5 pixel border around table

Rules between row and column groups

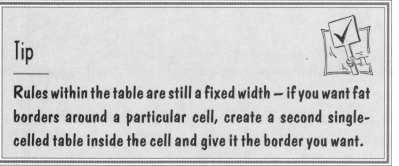

## Tip

Rules within the table are still a fixed width — if you want fat borders around a particular cell, create a second single-celled table inside the cell and give it the border you want.

# Tables for page layout

Besides their obvious use for presenting tabular information, tables are also the only reliable way of enhancing the layout of a page in browsers which don't support HTML 4.0. If you're not catering for pre-HTML 4.0 browsers, skip straight on to style sheets (Chapter 6) – if not, read on.

## Before you start

Make a plan. Decide more or less how you want your page to look – where you want images, where any accompanying text should fall, where you want empty space – and sketch it out. From this, you can work out how many tables you need, how many rows and columns each will have, and what needs to go in each cell.

## Planning tables

How do you break your sketch down? First, consider these points:

- A table is not displayed until the browser has read through the whole table code, so where possible, use a series of small tables rather than one large one, to save viewers staring at a blank screen for longer than necessary.

- Tables can't be put next to anything else, each new table starts on a new line – unless you embed it within the cell of another table.

- Cells can be merged together so that text or images are spread over more than one row and/or column – a 6 × 6 table does not have to consist of 36 identical boxes.

## Take note

It may seem horribly uncool in this digital age to revert to pen and paper, but it probably is the best thing to do at this stage, unless you have some DTP software such as PageMaker or Quark and prefer to play with this instead.

In our example, we'll start by separating the logo and introductory blurb from the rest; this can either be made into a very basic table, or more simply, we can just set **ALIGN=left** for the logo image. The next step is to draw a grid over the remaining part of the plan which encloses each distinct element in a cell. Don't worry about elements which span more than one cell in your grid for the moment – the important thing is that nothing gets missed out.

So, we see that we'll need to start with a table of three rows by six columns. Now we need to merge some of the cells together - I've numbered each cell on the picture below to make planning this stage easier.

● We have text spanning cells 2, 3, 4, and 5;

● two bits of text spanning cells 7 and 8, and cells 10 and 11;

● and more text spanning cells 13, 14, 15, and 16;

● we also have an image spanning cells 6, 12, and 18.

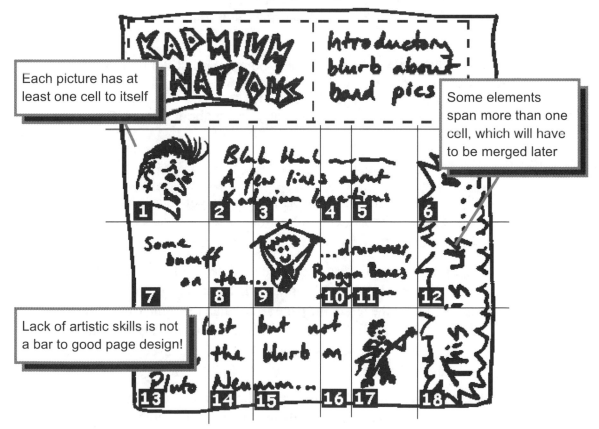

## Merging cells

The codes to merge cells are **COLSPAN=...** which sets the number of columns a cell spans, and **ROWSPAN =...**, which does the same for rows. These are placed inside the first cell to be merged. Blocks of cells can also be merged, by setting both **ROWSPAN** and **COLSPAN** values – but only rectangular blocks. You can't span 4 columns on one row and 3 on the next within the same **<TD>** block.

So, looking at our example, we would type **<TD COLSPAN=4>** at the beginning of cell 2 to merge it with cells 3, 4, and 5. When the browser reads the next **<TD...>** tag, it knows that you mean cell 6, not cell 3. In cell 6, we have an image which spans three cells vertically; this is done in exactly the same way: **<TD ROWSPAN=3>** reserves cells 12 and 18 for the contents of cell 6. The code for the first two rows of the table then, is:

```
<TR>
    <TD><IMG SRC="images/kadthmb1.gif"></TD>
    <TD COLSPAN=4>... a few lines about Kadmium Ignatious...</TD>
    <TD ROWSPAN=3><IMG SRC="images/band.gif"></TD>
</TR>
<TR>
    <TD COLSPAN=2>And now some bumff about the drummer,
Bagga Bones...</TD>
    <TD><IMG SRC="images/bagthmb1.gif"></TD>
    <TD COLSPAN=2>...and then a little more about him...</TD>
</TR>
```

## Empty cells

Normally, if you have a cell which is to be empty, you must type in the table data tags **<TD></TD>** anyway, so that the browser knows to skip over it. There are two exceptions to this, when you can just ignore the cell:

● If the cell is already reserved for the contents of another cell by the **COLSPAN** or **ROWSPAN** options. If for instance I put the 'This is us...' image on the left of the page rather than the right, (reserving cells 1,7 and 13 instead of 6, 12 and 18), then the first **<TD>** tag which the browser reads on the second row will be put in the second column (in cell 8 rather than cell 7).

● If the cell is at the end of a row. When the browser meets the **</TR>** tag, it ends the row, leaving the cells in any remaining columns blank.

## Take note

The source code for this — and all the other longer examples in this book — is available from the Made Simple Web site. Head to www.madesimple.co.uk and look for the Programming books.

<TD COLSPAN = 4> used for both of these blocks

<TD ROWSPAN = 3> to get this column

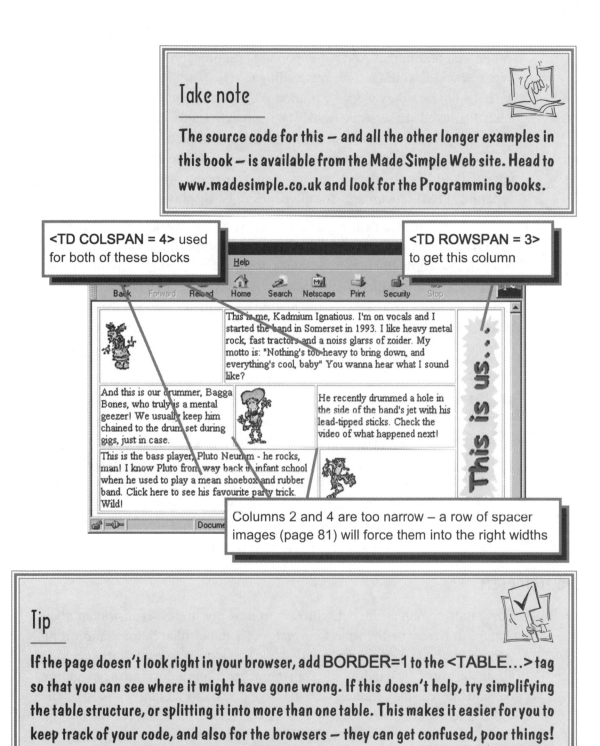

Columns 2 and 4 are too narrow – a row of spacer images (page 81) will force them into the right widths

## Tip

If the page doesn't look right in your browser, add BORDER=1 to the <TABLE...> tag so that you can see where it might have gone wrong. If this doesn't help, try simplifying the table structure, or splitting it into more than one table. This makes it easier for you to keep track of your code, and also for the browsers — they can get confused, poor things!

# Frames

When you add frames to a page, you are creating sub-windows inside the browser window. In fact, it's misleading to talk of adding frames to a page, as that's not how they work – a framed Web 'page' is actually several pages, each displayed in a separate frame. The master document for a frames-based page is just a shell, with no content. All it has is a set of instructions called a *frameset*, which tells the browser how to divide the window and which pages should be displayed in each frame to begin with. You then write separate HTML documents for the pages to be displayed in each frame.

Suppose that you want a navigation bar down the side, which visitors will use to find their way around your site. You need to build a frameset which splits the window vertically into two frames, a narrow one for the navigation bar and a wider one in which to display the various pages of your site. Then you write a new page to create your navigation bar with links from it to your other pages. These links will contain extra information specifying a *target frame* – this tells the browser in which frame to display the linked page.

There are two tags you need to create a frameset:

● **<FRAMESET...>** determines the size and shape of the frames. You may need several of these tags, as they can either divide the window into a number of **ROWS** or into **COLS**, but not both at the same time. The height or width of each row or column is set inside the **<FRAMESET...>** tag, either as a number of pixels, or as a percentage of the window size. The * character can be used to mean 'take up the rest of the space'.

● **<FRAME...>** assigns a **NAME** to each frame and gives the URL of the default page to be displayed in it – we'll come back to this in a moment.

## Nested framesets

For a more complex layout, you can to nest one frameset inside another. Again, this may be the time to sketch out a paper plan before embroiling yourself in code. For example, let's have a narrow frame containing a logo along the top of the window and split the larger frame below into a navigation bar and main display frame. First, the page is split horizontally into two. The top frame is defined as usual with a **<FRAME...>** tag; but for the bottom frame, we start a new **<FRAMESET...>**. This divides the frame into two columns, each defined with a **<FRAME...>**.

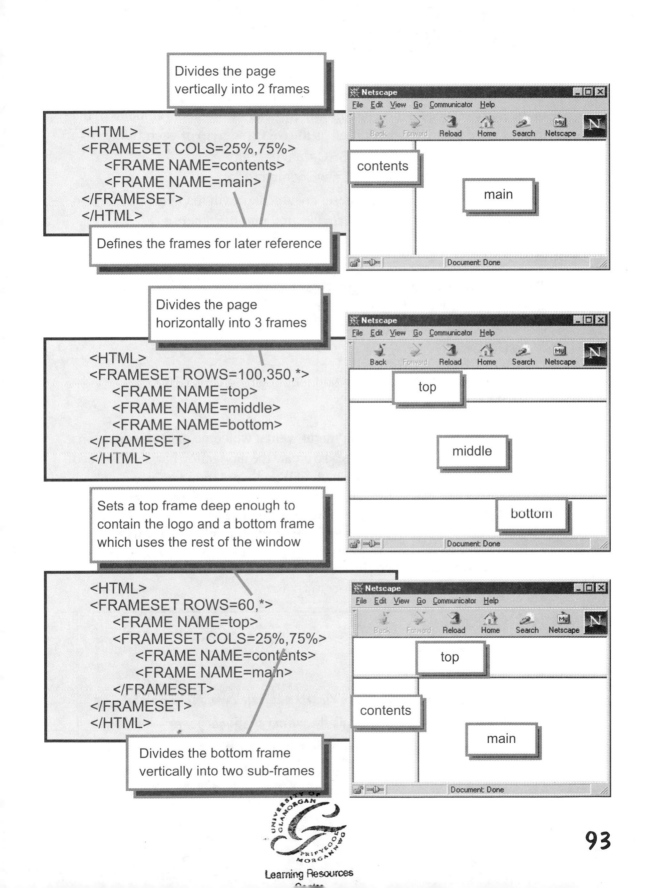

Divides the page vertically into 2 frames

```
<HTML>
<FRAMESET COLS=25%,75%>
   <FRAME NAME=contents>
   <FRAME NAME=main>
</FRAMESET>
</HTML>
```

Defines the frames for later reference

contents

main

Divides the page horizontally into 3 frames

```
<HTML>
<FRAMESET ROWS=100,350,*>
   <FRAME NAME=top>
   <FRAME NAME=middle>
   <FRAME NAME=bottom>
</FRAMESET>
</HTML>
```

top

middle

bottom

Sets a top frame deep enough to contain the logo and a bottom frame which uses the rest of the window

```
<HTML>
<FRAMESET ROWS=60,*>
   <FRAME NAME=top>
   <FRAMESET COLS=25%,75%>
      <FRAME NAME=contents>
      <FRAME NAME=main>
   </FRAMESET>
</FRAMESET>
</HTML>
```

Divides the bottom frame vertically into two sub-frames

top

contents

main

Learning Resources

# Filling in the frames

When you make the first link to a frames-based page, you just give the URL of the frameset document. The files which generate the actual contents of the frames have their URLs specified as the **SRC** (source) of each frame:

```
<FRAME NAME=contents SRC="navbar.htm" >
<FRAME NAME=main SRC="welcome.htm">
```

When a browser opens the frameset document, it will load *navbar.htm* into the frame called *contents* and *welcome.htm* into the other.

## Pages for small frames

The frame which holds the logo across the top of the window holds a very simple page – all it will be is an image, and perhaps some background and text colour information in the **<BODY...>** tag:

```
<HTML>
<BODY BGCOLOR=black>
    <CENTER><IMG SRC="kadmium3.gif"></CENTER>
</BODY>
</HTML>
```

For the main display frame, you might want a welcome page of some sort, or just launch straight into the site. To create the navigation bar, we just need a few images or pieces of text which will be linked to other pages:

```
<A HREF="home.htm"> <IMG SRC="homebut.gif"></A> <BR>
<A HREF="band.htm"><IMG SRC="bandbut.gif"></A> <BR>
<A HREF="tourdate.htm"><IMG SRC="gigbut.gif"></A> <BR>
...
```

The code given here will produce a page which looks fine – but doesn't work properly! Read on to find out how to fix it.

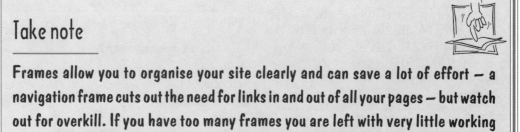

## Take note

Frames allow you to organise your site clearly and can save a lot of effort – a navigation frame cuts out the need for links in and out of all your pages – but watch out for overkill. If you have too many frames you are left with very little working space for the most important part of your page – the content. Make it simple.

# Links and targets

With a simple **<A HREF = >**, you'll find that the navigation bar is overwritten by the page which it is linked to. When you follow a normal link in a page *without* frames, the new page is displayed in the same window as the previous page. Frames normally work in just the same way. To avoid this, you must set a target frame for the link in the **<A HREF...>** tag:

```
<A HREF="tourdate.htm" TARGET=main>
```

Now, instead of displaying the page *tourdate.htm* in the navigation frame, the browser knows that it should put it in the frame called *main*.

As well as using named frames as targets, there are four special values which can be set for the **TARGET** option:

- **TARGET= _self** is not really needed, as it is the default. It tells the browser to display the new page in the current frame.

- **TARGET= _top** replaces the whole page, so that all frames are removed and the new page is displayed in the entire window.

- **TARGET= _parent** replaces the enclosing frameset, removing sub-divisions within it.

- **TARGET= _blank** spawns a new browser window and displays the page in it. This is often used if you include links to other sites on the Web from your page, so that people can go to those sites and browse from there without worrying about backtracking to your site, because yours is still there in a window underneath the new one they've been using.

## Base targets

For something like a navigation frame, pretty well all of the links will be targeted on the same frame. To save you typing in the same target for every link, you can set a **BASE TARGET** in the head of the page, which is used unless a different target is specifically defined for a particular link:

```
<HTML>
<HEAD>
   <BASE TARGET=main>
</HEAD>
<BODY>
```

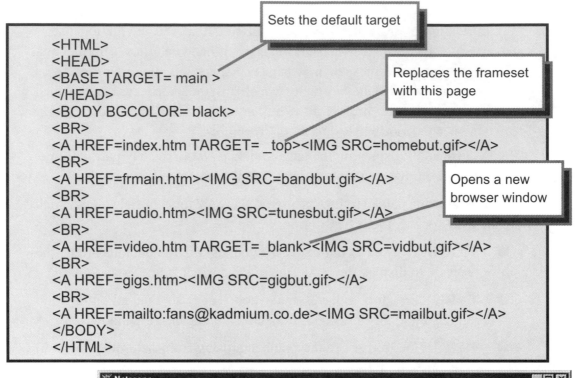

Sets the default target

Replaces the frameset with this page

Opens a new browser window

```
<HTML>
<HEAD>
<BASE TARGET= main >
</HEAD>
<BODY BGCOLOR= black>
<BR>
<A HREF=index.htm TARGET= _top><IMG SRC=homebut.gif></A>
<BR>
<A HREF=frmain.htm><IMG SRC=bandbut.gif></A>
<BR>
<A HREF=audio.htm><IMG SRC=tunesbut.gif></A>
<BR>
<A HREF=video.htm TARGET=_blank><IMG SRC=vidbut.gif></A>
<BR>
<A HREF=gigs.htm><IMG SRC=gigbut.gif></A>
<BR>
<A HREF=mailto:fans@kadmium.co.de><IMG SRC=mailbut.gif></A>
</BODY>
</HTML>
```

The Heavy Metal Rock God's
Shrine to Kadmium Ignatious

Home
The band
Tunes
Video
Gigs
Fan Email

## Error 999: File under investigation

The file you requested is currently under investigation by the Metropolitan Police, the Fraud Squad, Scotland Yard, the newly-appointed drugs tsar, Sherlock Holmes, the Famous Five and a real old dragon of a woman from the Passport Office.

The new page is displayed in a different frame – as long as it can be opened!

# Changing a frame's look

By default, frames have those slim silver edges and certain other properties which you may have come across as you've been exploring how they work. If a page is too big to fit in the frame, scroll bars will appear along the right-hand and/or bottom edges. If you move the cursor over a frame border, you'll find that it turns into a double-headed arrow, indicating that you can drag the border to resize the frame. All of these properties can be changed.

## Frame size and colour

The width of the frame's border can be set in the **<FRAMESET...>** tag:

```
<FRAMESET COLS=20%,80% BORDER=25>
```

To hide the borders completely, set the option **FRAMEBORDER = 0** (or **no**) – use **1** or **yes** to turn them on.

To change the colour, set **BORDERCOLOR=...** inside a **<FRAME...>** or **<FRAMESET...>** tag. If you have more than one frameset, you can have borders of different colours, but *all* borders in any one frameset will be the same colour. If you set conflicting instructions, the first is applied – here, the borders of the horizontal frameset will be blue, and the vertical ones yellow:

```
<FRAMESET ROWS=85,*,85>
    <FRAME NAME=top SRC="frbanner.htm" BORDERCOLOR=blue>
        <FRAMESET COLS=25%,25% BORDERCOLOR=yellow>
            <FRAME NAME=contents SRC="navbar.htm">
            <FRAME NAME=main SRC="frmain.htm">
        </FRAMESET>
            <FRAME NAME=bottom SRC="logo.htm" BORDERCOLOR=red>
</FRAMESET>
```

## Frame control

The **<FRAME...>** tag has two options to control the way the borders work:

● **NORESIZE** anchors *all* borders around that frame so visitors to your site cannot mess with your layout in their window.

● **SCROLLING= yes, no** or **auto** sets whether or not a frame has scroll bars. **auto** is the default and the most useful, as it adds scroll bars only if necessary – but if you don't want a great clunky thing popping up on the side of your nice neat frame, then you'll set it to **no**.

# Summary

❏ The standard text and image formatting tags give only limited control over the layout of a page. To specify layout more accurately, you need to use either tables or frames (or both).

❏ A table consists of a set of rows, made up of cells. The highest number of cells in a row fixes the number of columns in the table.

❏ The formatting options of the <TABLE> tag allow you to specify its width, alignment, background and the spacing around its cells.

❏ Internet Explorer has additional tables options, allowing you to add headers and footers, to group columns, and to control the display of the table's borders and the rules between cells.

❏ The COLSPAN and ROWSPAN options can be used to merge cells across columns or rows.

❏ Frames divide the browser window into independent areas. Though you can only divide either horizontally or vertically in any one frameset, they can be combined to produce a great variety of layouts.

❏ A named frame can be the target for a link, so that the linked document is displayed in it. The target can also be the linking document, its containing window or a new window.

❏ A frame can be of fixed size, and scroll bars can be turned on and off, if required.

# 6 Cascading Style Sheets

Style sheets . . . . . . . . . . . . . . . . 100

Elements and inheritance . . . . . . . .102

Font attributes . . . . . . . . . . . . . . .104

Text attributes . . . . . . . . . . . . . . .106

Colours and backgrounds . . . . . . . .108

Margins and borders . . . . . . . . . . . 110

Classes and IDs . . . . . . . . . . . . . . 112

Contained styles . . . . . . . . . . . . . . 114

Structured sheets . . . . . . . . . . . . . 115

Positioning elements . . . . . . . . . . . 117

External style sheets . . . . . . . . . . .120

Summary . . . . . . . . . . . . . . . . . .122

# Style sheets

Style sheets give you far more control over the appearance of your pages. Any formatting that can be done with tags, can also by done with style sheets, but additionally, style sheets allow you to:

- set text size and spacing – between letters, words and lines;
- set margins, borders and background colours for the page and for paragraphs – background colour can also be set *within* a paragraph;
- control the way images appear in the background of a page, and use images as bullets for lists.

Though there are a number of different style sheet languages, each extending HTML in its own special way, the one that is most important to most people at present is CSS1 – Cascading Style Sheets, version 1. Its standards have been implemented (in almost the same way) in Internet Explorer and Netscape Navigator, from version 4.0 onwards. It is 'cascading' in the sense that you can have any number of style sheets active within a page – a 'style sheet' is simply a definition of one or more styles – and formatting is passed on from one sheet to the next. The **<P>** tag, for instance, might have styles applied to it at, say, three points in a document. The first style sheet might set the colour, font size and margins; the second set the margins; the third set the colour and background colour. The final display will take the font size from the first, margins from the second and its colours from the third sheet.

This may sound as if there is unnecessary duplication going on here, but that's not so. Multiple style sheets, and restyling allow you to set different formats within a document. In large organisations, you can have one style sheet to set the basic common format for the whole site, a second to set the variations for a departments, a third to set special format to suit an individual document, and further restyling within it to pick out particular items.

## Take note

Unfortunately, style sheets are not yet standard. There are significant differences in the way that Internet Explorer and Navigator interpret style sheets, and browsers before version 4.0 cannot handle them at all.

# Specifying style sheets

There are three ways that you can add style to a document.

- Create a link to, or import, an external style sheet – the neatest approach when you want a common style for a set of pages. We'll look closer at this later (page 120).

- Use the **<STYLE>...</STYLE>** pair to enclose a set of styling lines. The block can be written anywhere in the document, but is normally placed in the **HEAD** area, where its formats will be applied to the whole page. Here's a simple **STYLE** block:

```
<STYLE TYPE=text/css>
    H1 { text-align:center; color: red }
</STYLE>
```

  The phrase **TYPE = text/css** is essential. It specifies the style sheet language – in this case Cascading Style Sheets. The style sheet language can be additionally specified in a **META** tag, at the top of the **HEAD**.

```
<META http-equiv="Content-Style-Type" content="text/css">
```

  The style definition line starts with the tag name – without <brackets> – and has one or more styles given as 'attribute:format', separated by semi-colons. The example line redefines **<H1>** so that it is centred and coloured red – but in the default font and size.

- Define a tag, within the **BODY** code, by using the **STYLE** keyword. The style only applies to that tagged element; e.g.

```
<P STYLE="color: blue">This paragraph is blue.</P>
<P>This is in the default paragraph colour.</P>
```

---

## Take note

‹STYLE› blocks can be written in the BODY area, but this creates problems. The code must be commented out to stop it being displayed when viewed by older browsers, and Navigator and Internet Explorer apply the styles differently.

# Elements and inheritance

In style sheet jargon, an *element* is a tag and the text or image affected by it. The BODY itself, an **<H…>** heading, a **<P>** paragraph, a **<B>bold</B>** item within a block of text – all are elements.

An element within another, such as bold text within a paragraph, is referred to as a *child* of the containing element – and this is its *parent*. In style sheets, as in life, children inherit characteristics from their parents. So, if the **<P>** tag has been defined as blue, 14 point, the **<B>** bold text is also blue and 14 point – unless these formats have been overridden by styling the **<B>** tag. (It will also be bold, from its HTML definition – unless this too has been overridden.)

The code and screenshots opposite are designed to show inheritance at work. Don't worry too much about the details of formatting at this stage, we'll get back to this shortly. The important thing to notice here is how styles are inherited and overriden.

● The **BODY** style sets white text on a black background, centre-aligned.

● **H1** has a different font and changes the text colour, but takes centre-alignment from the **BODY** setting.

● **P** sets black on yellow, with margins of 10% of the screen width – but still centre-aligned.

● **B** sets the background to blue and capitalises the text, but retains the text colour of its parent element – white within untagged text and black within the P element.

## Take note

Compare the screenshots opposite. Navigator (top) only changes the background colour beneath the text; Internet Explorer (bottom) takes the colour up to the margins. This is one of several differences in the way that the two browsers interpret style sheets.

## Parent and child elements

```
<HEAD>
<TITLE>Parent and Child Elements</TITLE>
<STYLE type=text/css>
    BODY {background-color:black; color:white; text-align:center}
    H1 {color:yellow; font-family: arial; font-size: 18pt}
    P {background-color:yellow;color:black; margin:10%}
    B {background-color:blue; text-transform:uppercase}
</STYLE>
</HEAD>
<BODY>
<H1>Elements - Parent and Child</H1>
Untagged text takes the <B>BODY </B>style
<P>The P tag now carries style information. Its colour settings override those
of BODY, but it keeps the BODY alignment as this has not been redefined.
<P>An element inside another is its child. <B> B is a child of P. </B> It
inherits P's characteristics, but adds some of its own.</P>
</BODY>
</HTML>
```

Styles are set by the **attribute:format** expression

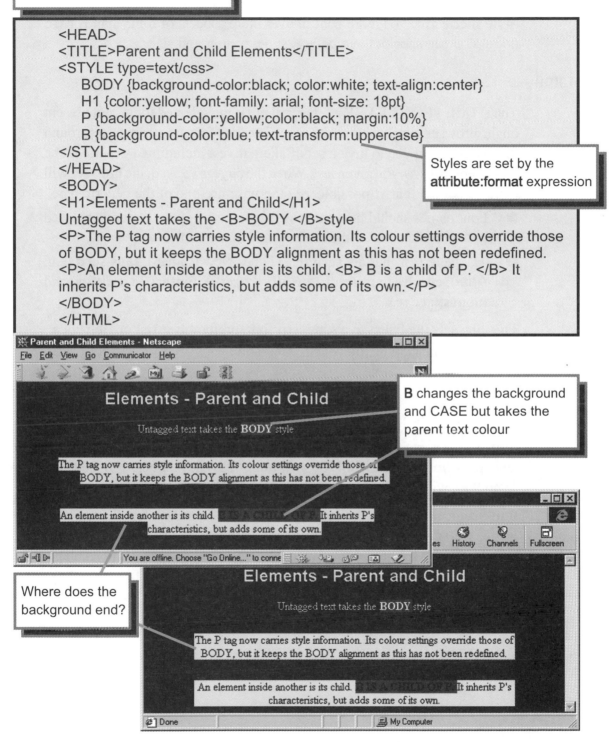

B changes the background and CASE but takes the parent text colour

Where does the background end?

# Font attributes

Style sheets give you more control over more aspects of fonts than HTML does. You can specify the typeface, style, weight and size.

## font-family

The HTML **<FONT FACE = >** tag will fail if the selected font is not present on the browser that is viewing the page. The font-family: attribute gets round this by allowing you to give a set of alternatives, including a generic name – this should always be given last. When the page is viewed, the browser will match a named font, if possible, or otherwise use one of the generic type.

● Font names should be written as they appear in your system, enclosed in "double quotes" if there are spaces in the name.

● The generic names are **serif** (e.g. Times New Roman), **sans-serif** (e.g. Arial), **cursive** (e.g. *Lucida Calligraphy*), **fantasy** (e.g. Playbill) and **monospace** (e.g. Courier New).

This line sets the P text to a sans serif font, preferably Arial or Helvetica.

P {font-family: arial, helvetica, sans-serif}

## Other attributes

**font-style** can be italic, normal or oblique (not implemented by Navigator).

**font-weight** gives you many levels of 'boldness'. It can be set by the keywords **normal, bold, bolder** or **lighter**, or by the numbers 100, 200, 300 … to 900, with 500 being normal and 900 the heaviest type.

**font-size** can be set by the keywords **xx-small, x-small, small, medium, large, x-large** or **xx-large** (equivalent to HTML sizes 1 to 7), or **larger** or **smaller** (which set the size relative to the parent element), or by a percentage. This latter is based on the line-height – see page 106.

e.g. to make the H2 headings italic, a fairly heavy bold, size 5:

H2 {font-style:italic; font-weight:700; font-size:large}

Use commas to separate names in font-family lists

```
<HEAD>
<TITLE>Fonts in style sheets</TITLE>
<STYLE type=text/css>
    BODY {font-family: "Book Antiqua", Garamond, serif}
    H1 {font-family: "Lucida Calligraphy"; font-size:18pt}
    H2 {font-style:italic; font-size:large}
    P {font-family:sans-serif; font-size:14pt; font-weight:600}
    B {font-weight:bolder}
    I {font-style:normal; font-weight:lighter}
</STYLE>
</HEAD>
<BODY>
<H1>Corporate SwimSuits</H1>
<H2>Do you have a <B>company pool?</B></H2>
<P>We can supply swimsuits decorated with <B STYLE = font-size:
larger>your company logo</B>
<P>In all sizes from <I>Typist</I> to <B>Managing Director</B>
</BODY>
</HTML>
```

Semicolons between attributes where several are set in one line

Inline style setting

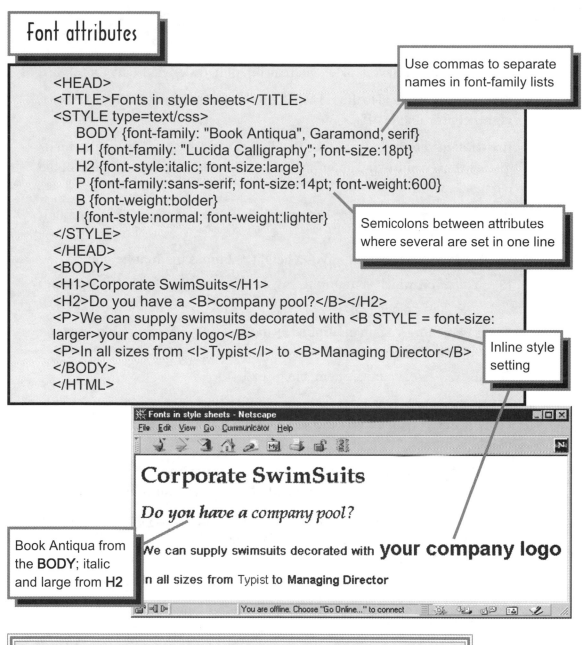

Book Antiqua from the **BODY**; italic and large from **H2**

## Corporate SwimSuits

*Do you have a company pool?*

We can supply swimsuits decorated with **your company logo**

In all sizes from Typist to **Managing Director**

## Take note

CSS is unforgiving of errors. Any mistakes in the punctuation or spelling of attribute names or definitions and the style will not be applied.

# Text attributes

These relate to the layout of text and can be applied alongside any font styles.

**text-align** is identical to the HTML **ALIGN** option, taking the keyword **left**, **right**, **center** and **justify**.

**text-indent** sets the indent of the first line of a paragraph. The length can be given in em (width of the letter 'm'), cm, px (pixels) or as a percentage of the element's width.

**line-height** sets the distance between the baselines of text in a paragraph. It can be given as:

- the keyword **normal**, gives a height 1.2 times the font height.
- a *number*, which is multiplied by the font size; e.g. for 1° line-spacing:

    P {line-height:1.5}

- a *percentage*, again multiplied by the font size; e.g. for double-spacing:

    P {line-height:200%}

- a *fixed size*, in units of em, cm or px.

When the line height is given as a number, the line height in any child elements are multiplied by the same number; in other cases, the resultant height is inherited.

**text-decoration** has four possible settings. **underline** and **line-through**; **overline** (Internet Explorer only); and **blink** (Navigator only).

**text-transform** sets the case of characters, using the keywords **capitalize** (capital first letter only), **uppercase**, **lowercase** or **none**.

## Internet Explorer extras

IE 4.0 can also handle these attributes for fine-tuning the display:

**word-spacing** sets the distance between words, and is given as **normal** or a length in em.

**letter-spacing** likewise sets the distance between letters in a word.

**vertical-align** sets the position of the text in relation to the baseline – this is most visible where tagged text is embedded in a paragraph. There are several keywords of which only **sub** (subscript) and **super** (superscript) have any noticeable effect.

106

## Text attributes

```
<HEAD>
<TITLE>Text attributes</TITLE>
<STYLE type=text/css>
    BODY {text-align:center}
    H1 {text-transform:capitalize; text-decoration:underline}
    P {text-align:left; text-indent:2cm;font-size:10pt; line-height:180%}
</STYLE>
</HEAD>
<BODY>
<BR>
<H1>computer systems - statement</H1>
<P>In an article in this publication on the 29th February 1999, we may
have given the misleading impression that <B>Computer Systems Inc</
B> (registered office Joe's Dive, Pirate Creek, Cocoa Islands, Lesser
Antilles) are a bunch of incompetent, unprincipled, money-grabbing
sharks whose business activities would be criminal if practised in any
country with a half-way decent judicial system. After discussions with
their advisers, Big Al and the boys, we unreservedly withdraw anything
that we said that may have given such an impression.
</BODY>
</HTML>
```

Sets initial capitals

Left-aligned, deep indent, small text, well-spaced lines,

The **BODY** centre-alignment affects the heading; the paragraph is set to left-aligned

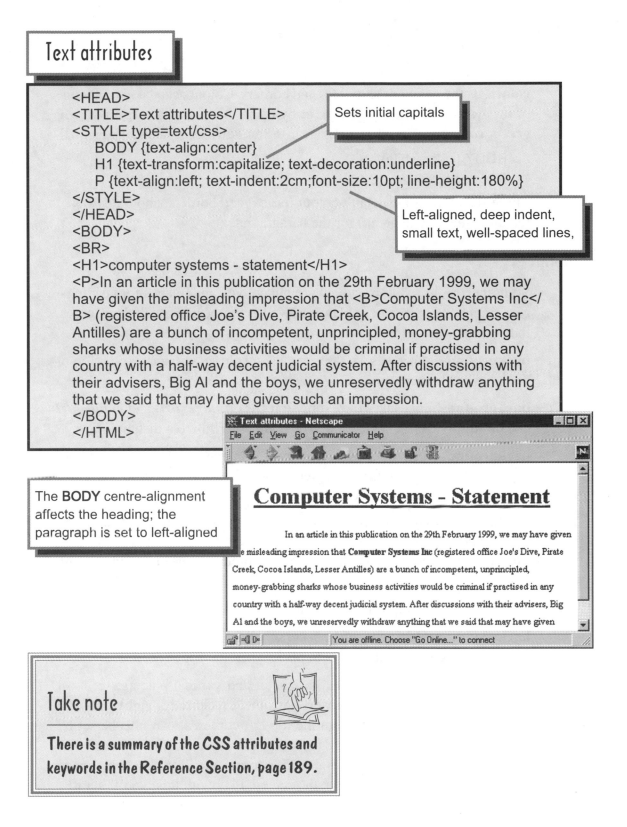

Text attributes - Netscape

File  Edit  View  Go  Communicator  Help

# Computer Systems - Statement

In an article in this publication on the 29th February 1999, we may have given the misleading impression that **Computer Systems Inc** (registered office Joe's Dive, Pirate Creek, Cocoa Islands, Lesser Antilles) are a bunch of incompetent, unprincipled, money-grabbing sharks whose business activities would be criminal if practised in any country with a half-way decent judicial system. After discussions with their advisers, Big Al and the boys, we unreservedly withdraw anything that we said that may have given

You are offline. Choose "Go Online..." to connect

## Take note

There is a summary of the CSS attributes and keywords in the Reference Section, page 189.

# Colours and backgrounds

**color** sets the colour of text, lines and borders. Colours can be given as one of the standard names (page 30), or by using the expression **rgb(*red_val, green_val, blue_val*)**. The values are in the range 0 to 255 – not hexadecimal.

```
BODY {color:white}
P {color:rgb(192,0,192)}
```

These set white as the default colour for text and borders, and lilac (lots of red and blue, but no green) for the paragraph text.

## Backgrounds

Style sheets allow you to set background colours and images for headings, paragraphs and other blocks of text, as well as for the page itself. In all cases, the attributes are set in the same way.

**background-color** takes a colour name, an **rgb(*val,val,val*)** expression or the keyword **transparent**.

**background-image** takes the expression **URL(*image_url*)** and *image_url* can be simply the filename, or a Web address to link to a distant image.

**background-repeat** defines the way that the image is shown. The keyword **repeat** sets full screen tiling; **repeat-x** duplicates in across top; **repeat-y** produces a strip down the left; **no-repeat** sets a single image.

```
BODY {background-image: URL(logo.gif); background-repeat:repeat;
background-color:silver}
```

This tiles the screen with the logo image, or colours it pale grey if images are not loaded by the browser.

Internet Explorer can handle two other options:

**background-attachment** can be set to **scroll**, so that the image moves with the text, or **fixed**, so that it stays in place when the page is scrolled.

**background-position** takes the horizontal and vertical placing, set most simply by the keywords **top, center, bottom**, **left, center** or **right**, or by the length in cm or px (pixels) from the top left corner. It can also be set by percentages. These are relative to both the image and the browser. For example, 25% 75% means the point 25% across and 75% down the image is set 25% across and 75% down the screen. Play with this, you'll get it!

Repeating image on the page background

```
<HEAD>
<TITLE>Backgrounds</TITLE>
<STYLE type=text/css>
  BODY {background-image:URL(Y2Kback.gif); background-repeat:repeat}
  H1 {background-image:URL(redback.gif); color:white}
  P {color:red;font-size:large}
  ADDRESS {background-color:rgb(192,192,0)); color:black}
</STYLE>
</HEAD>
<BODY>
<BR>
<H1>! Chaos Survival Secrets !</H1>
<P>Come the Year 2000 chaos will envelop the earth. Can you survive?
<P>For the secrets of survival, join the Y2K Cult.
<ADDRESS>E-mail the Cult Guardian at: nutter@endoftheworld.com
</ADDRESS>
</BODY>
</HTML>
```

Image on **<H1>** background

Images for text are repeated across the screen by IE 4.0, but not by Navigator

Imaged placed over to the right and vertically centred by **background-position:75% 50%**

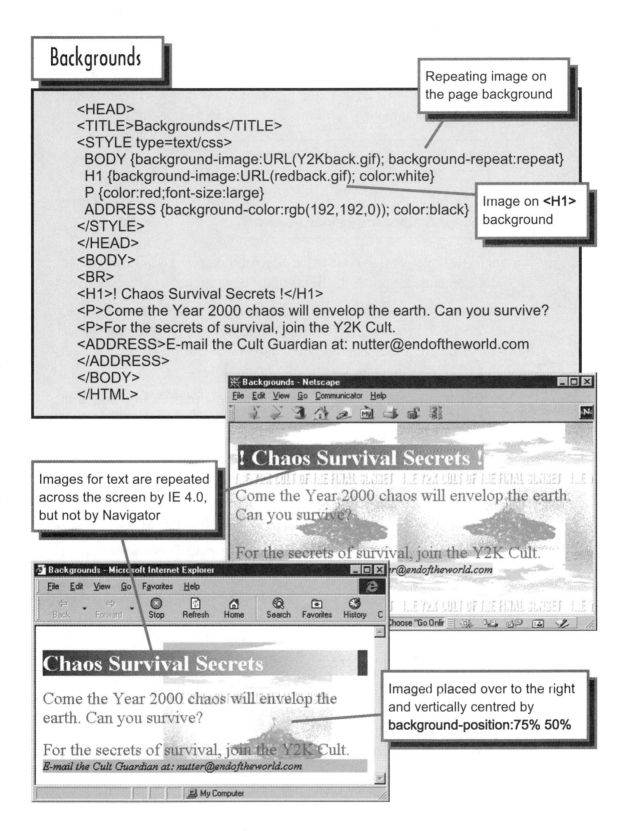

# Margins and borders

All *block elements* – the BODY, images, tables, headings, **<P>** and other tags that create paragraphs – have margins, borders and padding.

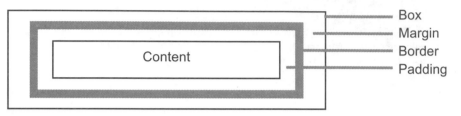

For the BODY element, the box is the edge of the screen window or page; for other elements, the box is the limits of the content of the parent element.

You can also use the attributes **width** and **height** to set the size of the box. Values are given in the usual cm, em or px units, or as a percentage of the limits of the parent element. In Navigator these can be applied to text elements as well as to images.

The margin, border and padding all have *width,* which can be anything from zero upwards. If there is no border, the combined margin and padding values determine the amount of space around the content. The simplest approach is to set all four sides the same. e.g.

    P {margin:10%; border-width:5px; padding:0.2cm}

This gives <P> paragraphs a margin all round of 10%, a border of 5 pixels, and padding of 0.2cm. Note that you must specify **border-width**.

Up to four values can be given to set different widths. With **margin** or **padding**, these are in the order top, right, bottom, left, and if only two or three are given, the missing values are taken from the opposite sides.

    P {margin: 5% 10%; padding:0.2cm 0.5cm 0.1cm}

This sets top and bottom margins of 5%, left and right margins of 10% and padding of 0.2cm at the top, 0.5cm to left and right and 0.1cm at the bottom.

**border-width** can also take one, two, three or four values, allocated to the sides as they are with padding.

You can also define individual sides by specifying **margin-top**, **border-width-bottom**, **padding-right**, etc., e.g.

    P {margin-top:10%; border-width-left:5px; padding-bottom:0.2cm}

# Border colour and style

The **border-color** attribute sets the colour of the whole border; sides can also be coloured individually by **border-top-color**, **border-left-color**, etc.

**border-style** can be set to **solid**, **double**, **groove**, **ridge**, **inset**, **outset** or **none** – and you need widths of 6px or more to see most of these effects.

```
<HEAD>
<TITLE>Margins and borders</TITLE>
<STYLE type=text/css>
    BODY {margin-top:0.1cm 5% 0.1cm 5%;
        border-width:0.5cm; border-style:groove;
        padding:1em; text-align:center}
    H1 {border-color:red;border-width:8 16 8 16; border-style:inset;
        color:red; padding:0.5cm}
    P {width:80%;border-width:6px; border-style:double;
        padding:0.1cm}
</STYLE>
</HEAD>
<BODY>
<H1>Come to Sunny Spain</H1>
<P>Where the se&ntilde;oritas are as hot as the sun, and the se&ntilde;ors
as fresh as the oranges!
</BODY>
</HTML>
```

Top and bottom margins set to 0.1cm; left and right set to 5%

**px** assumed, units not given

Definitions can spread over several lines

**border-width 8 16** has the same effect

**&ntilde;** produces 'ñ'

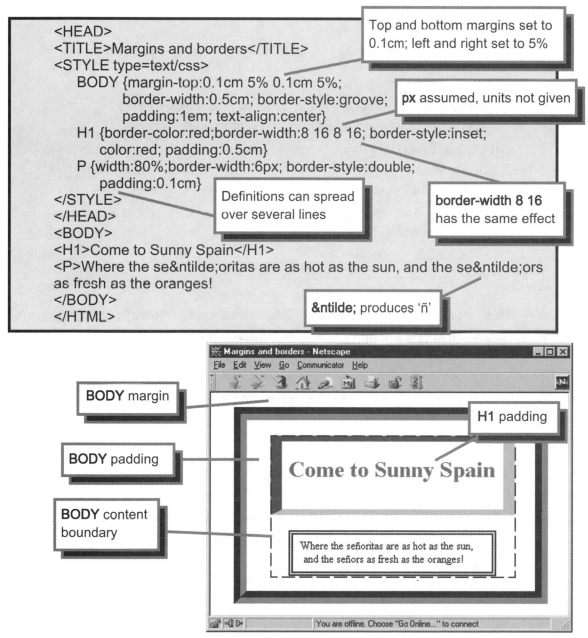

BODY margin

BODY padding

BODY content boundary

H1 padding

Come to Sunny Spain

Where the señoritas are as hot as the sun, and the señors as fresh as the oranges!

# Classes and IDs

Classes and IDs bring infinite variety to pages, as they allow you to apply any number of styles to the same basic HTML tag. Let's start with class. These definitions in the **STYLE** area …

```
H1 {font-size:30pt; color:green}
H1.redone {font-style:italic; color:red}
H1.blueone {color:blue}
```

… give you three variations on the **<H1>** tag. Within the **BODY** they are used like this:

```
<H1>This heading is 30 point in green</H1>
<H1 CLASS = redone>This is 30 point in red italics</H1>
<H1 CLASS = blueone>This is 30 point in blue, roman</H1>
```

All classes of **<H1>** inherit the default settings for the tag and any styles applied to the basic tag, though not from other classes. A class's definitions override any inherited ones.

A class defined for one tag cannot be applied to another. Given the examples above, this would not work …

```
<P CLASS = redone> …
```

## all classes

Here's one way to create formats that can be applied to any tags. A class definition applied to **all** can be used with any tag.

```
all.lightgreen {font-weight:300; color:green}
…
<H3 CLASS = lightgreen>A light green heading</H3>
<P CLASS = lightgreen>with text to match
```

## ID

This also allows you to create a format that can be applied to any tag. Define it in the **STYLE** area – note the # before the name:

```
#redbox {border-color:red; border-width:10px; padding:5px}
```

Apply as required, using the **ID** keyword and the name, without the #:

```
<H2 ID = redbox>This is important</H2>
…
<ADDRESS ID = redbox>Created by Wee Jimmy</ADDRESS>
```

## Class and ID

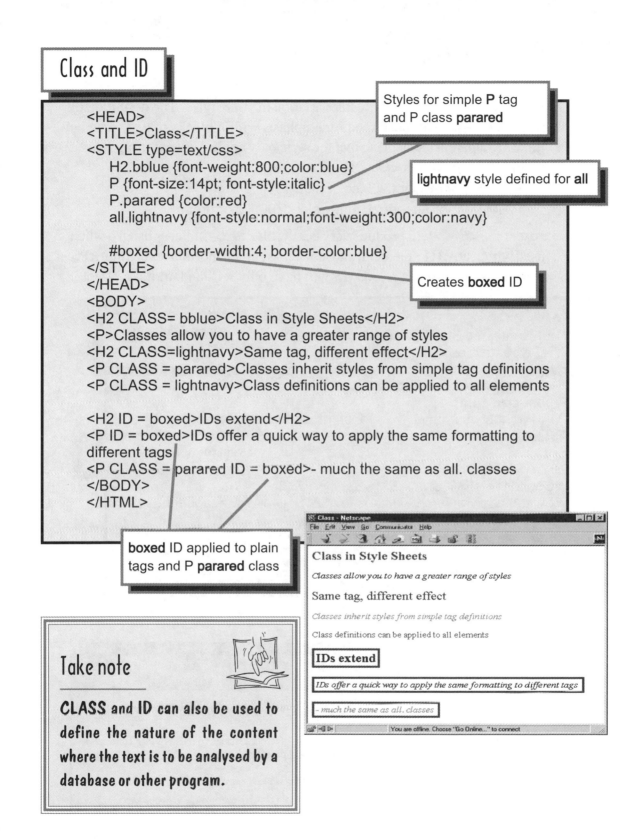

Styles for simple **P** tag and P class **parared**

**lightnavy** style defined for **all**

Creates **boxed** ID

```
<HEAD>
<TITLE>Class</TITLE>
<STYLE type=text/css>
    H2.bblue {font-weight:800;color:blue}
    P {font-size:14pt; font-style:italic}
    P.parared {color:red}
    all.lightnavy {font-style:normal;font-weight:300;color:navy}

    #boxed {border-width:4; border-color:blue}
</STYLE>
</HEAD>
<BODY>
<H2 CLASS= bblue>Class in Style Sheets</H2>
<P>Classes allow you to have a greater range of styles
<H2 CLASS=lightnavy>Same tag, different effect</H2>
<P CLASS = parared>Classes inherit styles from simple tag definitions
<P CLASS = lightnavy>Class definitions can be applied to all elements

<H2 ID = boxed>IDs extend</H2>
<P ID = boxed>IDs offer a quick way to apply the same formatting to
different tags
<P CLASS = parared ID = boxed>- much the same as all. classes
</BODY>
</HTML>
```

**boxed** ID applied to plain tags and P **parared** class

### Take note

CLASS and ID can also be used to define the nature of the content where the text is to be analysed by a database or other program.

---

**Class - Netscape**

File Edit View Go Communicator Help

**Class in Style Sheets**

*Classes allow you to have a greater range of styles*

Same tag, different effect

*Classes inherit styles from simple tag definitions*

Class definitions can be applied to all elements

| IDs extend |

| *IDs offer a quick way to apply the same formatting to different tags* |

| *- much the same as all. classes* |

You are offline. Choose "Go Online..." to connect

# Contained styles

Here is another way to get greater variation in your styles. The definition of inline tags – such as those used for emphasis within blocks of text – can be linked to a parent element, so that the style only applies when the tag is used within that parent. For example,

```
H1 EM  {font-weight:900;color:blue}
P EM {font-style:normal; font-weight:700; color:green}
```

After this, **<EM>** will produce very heavy, blue text – italic, as usual – when used within an **<H1>** element, and less heavy, green, normal text within **<P>** element. Used elsewhere, **<EM>** will have only its standard italic effect.

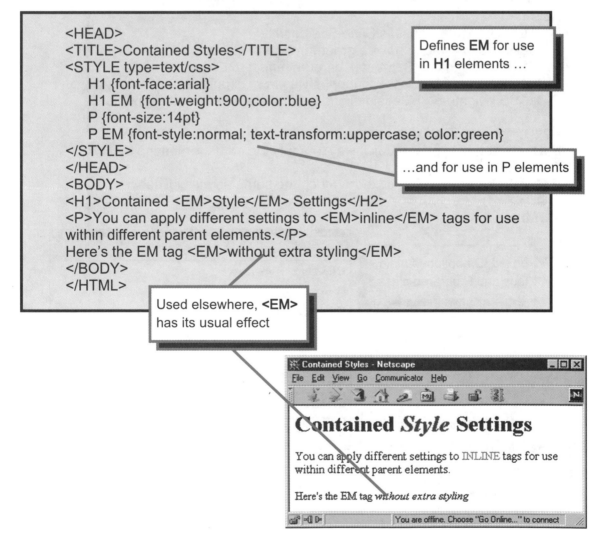

```
<HEAD>
<TITLE>Contained Styles</TITLE>
<STYLE type=text/css>
    H1 {font-face:arial}
    H1 EM  {font-weight:900;color:blue}
    P {font-size:14pt}
    P EM {font-style:normal; text-transform:uppercase; color:green}
</STYLE>
</HEAD>
<BODY>
<H1>Contained <EM>Style</EM> Settings</H2>
<P>You can apply different settings to <EM>inline</EM> tags for use
within different parent elements.</P>
Here's the EM tag <EM>without extra styling</EM>
</BODY>
</HTML>
```

Defines **EM** for use in **H1** elements …

…and for use in P elements

Used elsewhere, **<EM>** has its usual effect

Contained Styles - Netscape
File  Edit  View  Go  Communicator  Help

## Contained *Style* Settings

You can apply different settings to INLINE tags for use within different parent elements.

Here's the EM tag *without extra styling*

You are offline. Choose "Go Online..." to connect

# Structured sheets

Style sheets introduce two new tags for formatting sections of code.

## <DIV> </DIV>

**<DIV>** does nothing of itself, but acts as a container, marking off a division of the page in which a special format can be applied. It can be used as a simple HTML tag:

```
<DIV ALIGN = center>
    ... text and images all centred in here ...
</DIV>
```

It can take **STYLE** specifications. This line sets up a section in which the text is right-aligned and coloured red (unless overridden by the styles of elements within it).

```
<DIV STYLE = text-align:right;color:red>
```

**DIV** can also be formatted through a class or ID defined in the STYLE area.

```
DIV.cent {text-align:centre; font-size:16pt; font-style:italic}
...
<DIV CLASS = cent>
    text will be centred, italic in 16 point (unless overridden)
</DIV>
```

Exactly the same effect could be achieved by using an ID, though with that approach the same ID style could also be applied to any other suitable tag.

```
#cent {text-align:centre; font-size:16pt; font-style:italic}
...
<DIV ID = cent>
```

## <SPAN> </SPAN>

Like **<DIV>** this acts purely as a container, but in this case it marks off sections *within* text, and can only be used with style sheet formatting, e.g.

```
Stop when the lights are <SPAN STYLE = color:red>red</SPAN>
```

**SPAN** can be defined through a class or ID, in just the same way as **DIV**.

```
SPAN.shout {font-size:18pt; font-weight:800}
...
This is really <SPAN CLASS = shout>important</SPAN>
```

## SPAN and DIV

```
<HTML>
<HEAD>
<TITLE>Div and Span</TITLE>
 <STYLE type=text/css>
  P {font-size:18pt; font-face:arial}
  SPAN.initial { font-size:30pt;font-face:serif }
  DIV.publisher{color:green; font-style:italic; font-size:14pt; border-width:10}
 </STYLE>
</HEAD>
<BODY>
<DIV STYLE = color:red>
  <P><SPAN class=initial>O</SPAN>nce upon a time there was a Web
and it was <SPAN STYLE = font-size:10pt>very small...</P></SPAN>
</DIV>

This exciting tale of how an itsy-bitsy spider span a little web and span it
some more until it covered the whole world wide, is available from all
good bookstores or direct from

<DIV CLASS=publisher ALIGN = center>
  <P>The <SPAN class=initial>C</SPAN>ave of <SPAN class=initial>
S</SPAN>illy <SPAN class=initial>S</SPAN>tories</P>
</DIV>
</BODY>
</HTML>
```

> SPAN and DIV classes defined

> DIV sets colour to red

> Inline SPAN definition

> Unformatted text

> SPAN.initial class used for initials

### Take note

DIV and SPAN are also used for structuring text for analysis by databases and other software.

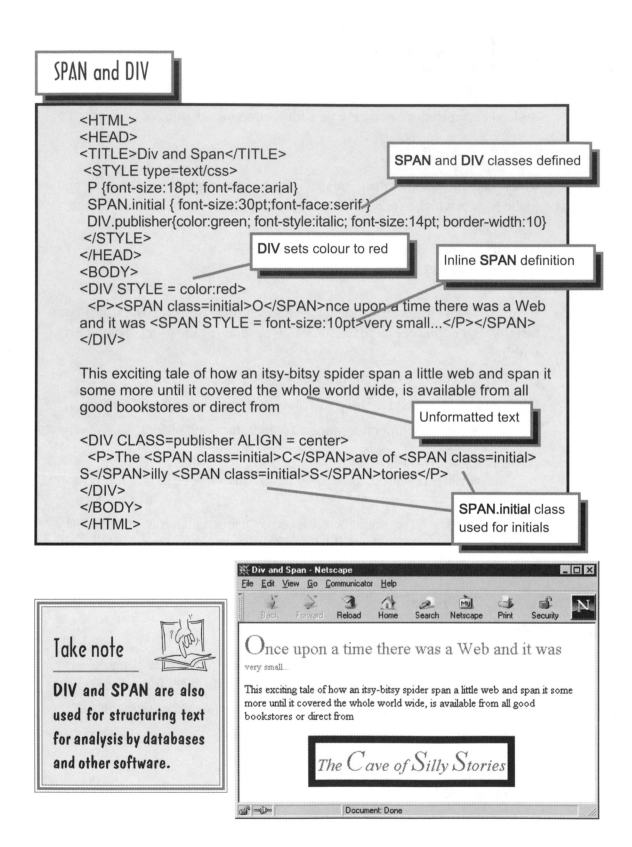

Div and Span - Netscape

File  Edit  View  Go  Communicator  Help

Back  Forward  Reload  Home  Search  Netscape  Print  Security

Once upon a time there was a Web and it was

very small...

This exciting tale of how an itsy-bitsy spider span a little web and span it some more until it covered the whole world wide, is available from all good bookstores or direct from

*The Cave of Silly Stories*

Document: Done

# Positioning elements

Style sheets give you two new ways to set the position of elements. The **float** and **clear** attributes provide a quick and easy way to align images and text; while the use of layers gives you far more accurate positioning of any elements at the cost of rather more work.

## Float and clear

**float** aligns an image to the left or right of the window, and can be combined with margin-left or margin-right to place it more accurately. It's not actually much use by itself as any subsequent text will normally be printed directly after the start of it – with the effect the image 'floats' on top of the text. To stop this, you must set the **clear** attribute. This determines whether clear space is needed for displaying text. There are four settings:

- **none** says display text beside – or between – floating images.
- **left** and **right** insists there must be clear space to the left (right). The text starts printing on the next line below the floating image.
- **both** holds the display until there are no floating elements either side.

## Layers

The basic concept behind layers is simple – by adding position information to a tag, you locate an element anywhere on screen. These elements are displayed in the order that they appear in the code, with later ones overlapping earlier – hence the name 'layer'. In theory, you can set a position on any tag. In practice, it only seems to work properly with **<DIV>** and **<SPAN>**. This is no great problem – if you wanted to locate a multi-line block of text, you'd have to use **<DIV>**, and it just means two extra lines round images.

The hard work is getting things in the right place! If you are very organised, you can plan the layout, but trial and error gets you there in the end. (And don't forget that if the page is going onto the Web, people will be viewing it in a wide range of window sizes.)

**position** can be set **absolute** – measured from the top left of the window or of its containing element (**DIV**s can be nested) – or **relative** – measured from the bottom left corner of the previous layer. The **top** and **left** distances can be given in the usual choice of em, cm and px units.

You can define the layer as a class in the **STYLE** area:

DIV.flow {position:absolute; top:200px; left:300px}

or directly within the **<DIV>** tag

<DIV STYLE=position:absolute; top:100px; left:100px>

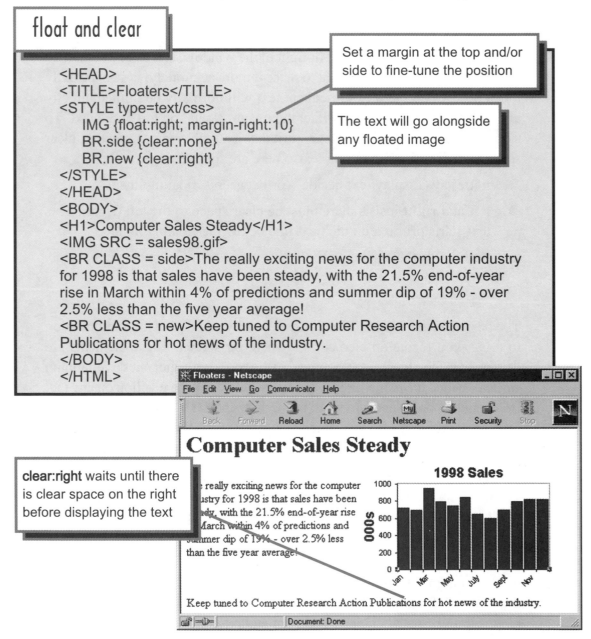

## float and clear

```
<HEAD>
<TITLE>Floaters</TITLE>
<STYLE type=text/css>
    IMG {float:right; margin-right:10}
    BR.side {clear:none}
    BR.new {clear:right}
</STYLE>
</HEAD>
<BODY>
<H1>Computer Sales Steady</H1>
<IMG SRC = sales98.gif>
<BR CLASS = side>The really exciting news for the computer industry
for 1998 is that sales have been steady, with the 21.5% end-of-year
rise in March within 4% of predictions and summer dip of 19% - over
2.5% less than the five year average!
<BR CLASS = new>Keep tuned to Computer Research Action
Publications for hot news of the industry.
</BODY>
</HTML>
```

Set a margin at the top and/or side to fine-tune the position

The text will go alongside any floated image

**clear:right** waits until there is clear space on the right before displaying the text

**Floaters - Netscape**

File Edit View Go Communicator Help

Back  Forward  Reload  Home  Search  Netscape  Print  Security  Stop

# Computer Sales Steady

really exciting news for the computer ustry for 1998 is that sales have been dy, with the 21.5% end-of-year rise March within 4% of predictions and summer dip of 19% - over 2.5% less than the five year average!

**1998 Sales**

Keep tuned to Computer Research Action Publications for hot news of the industry.

Document: Done

Colours and borders can be applied to **DIV**s – here they've been set on **P** so that the same style can be used in two layers.

```
<TITLE>Layers</TITLE>
<STYLE type=text/css>
    H1 {text-align:center}
    B  {font-weight:800; font-size:14pt; color:red}
    P  {border-width:5px; border-color:red; background-color:yellow}
    DIV.pic {position:absolute; top:50px; left:50px}
    DIV.flow {position:absolute; top:200px; left:300px}
</STYLE>
</HEAD>
<BODY>
<H1>Cash is Safer than Savings</H1>

<DIV CLASS = pic> <IMG SRC = loss.gif> </DIV>

<DIV STYLE="position:absolute; top:100px; left:100px; margin:25px">
<P>Come the millenium when all systems fail, thy gold shall flow from
thy bank account in a tide of loss.
<BR>Not literally of course, it would have to be <B>REALLY</B> hot to
do that
</DIV>

<DIV CLASS = flow>
<P> Flow ... flow ... flow ... </P>
</DIV>
</BODY>
</HTML>
```

Positions can be set in the **STYLE** area …

… and in the **DIV** tag

## Take note

**Netscape supports a LAYER tag that allows much more control over positioning – but as IE 4.0 does not recognise this, it's not (yet) suitable for general use.**

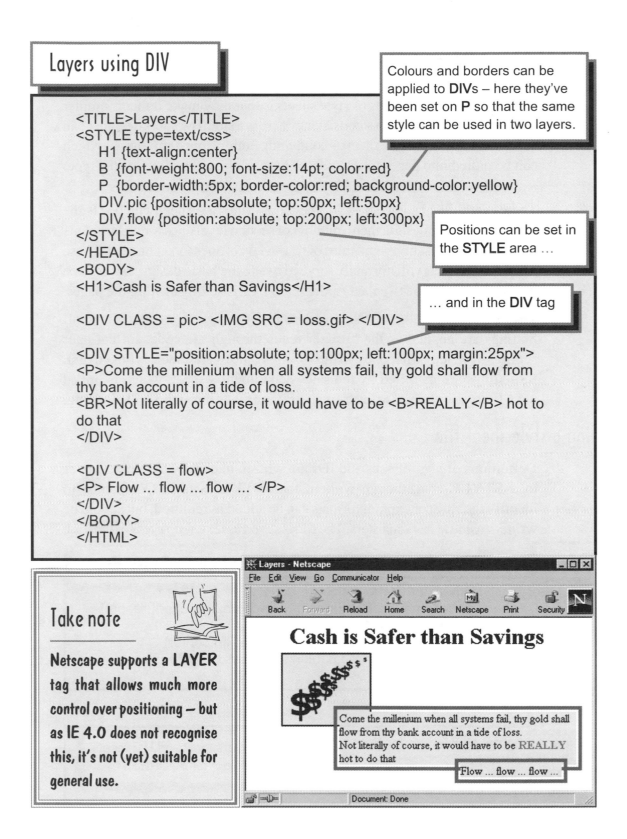

119

# External style sheets

One of the key advantages of style sheets is that they make it much simpler to create – and to maintain – consistency across a site. The site's designer can set up free-standing style sheets – containing nothing but definitions – which can be pulled into pages to set styles. These are linked by lines of the type:

<LINK REL=STYLESHEET TYPE=text/css HREF=corp.css>

There might just be one sheet for the whole site, or a sheet which sets the overall corporate design, then a number of second level ones for departments within the organisation – and third or fourth levels ones too, if needed. These lower level sheets will normally serve to tweak the basic design, not replace it. The design can be tweaked further by **STYLE** settings within the pages.

The order in which the **<LINK>** and **<STYLE>** tags are written is crucial! Settings are applied as the browser reads through the code, so that later settings override earlier ones. In this example, the overall sheet is linked first. Its settings are modified by the sales department's sheet, which is linked next. Final adjustments to the formats are then made through STYLE setting.

## Creating a style sheet file

Definitions of tags, classes and IDs are written in exactly the same way as in a **STYLE** area, though without the **<STYLE>** tags. Comments, to identify the sheet or explain formats can be added as required, but should be written inside **/\* … \*/** markers. The file is saved as text, with a **.css** extension.

**corp.css**

Sets the firm's basic style

```
/* corporate style sheet for Corporate Swim Suits */
    BODY {background-image:URL(shorts.gif); background-repeat:repeat}
    P {font-size:14pt; margin-left:10px; margin-right:20px}
    H1, H2, H3, H4 {font-family:arial,sans-serif; text-align:center}
    ADDRESS {background-color:red;padding:5px; border-width:5px;
border-color:blue}
```

**sales.css**

```
/* departmental style sheet for Sales */
    P {color:red}
    H1 {color:navy}
    ADDRESS {border-color:navy}
```

Sets colours for **P** and **H1**; resets border colour for **ADDRESS**

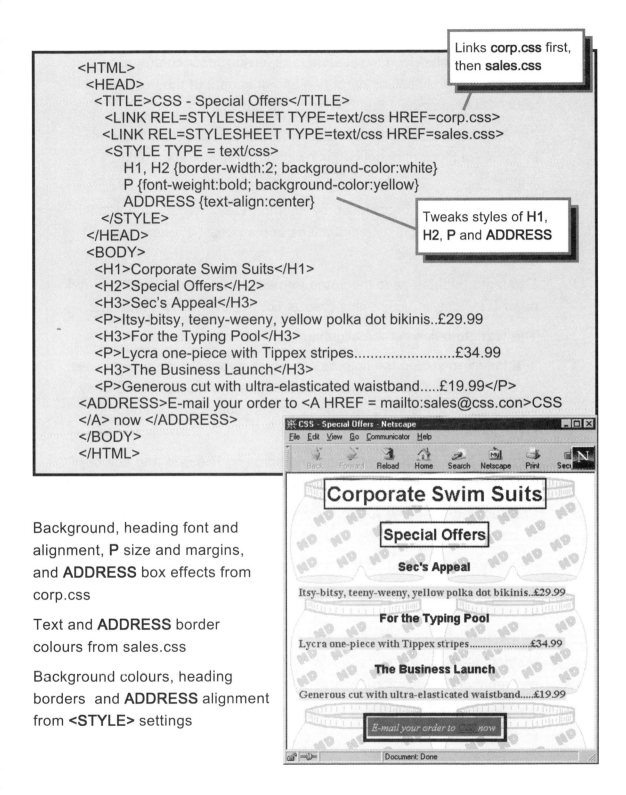

```
<HTML>
 <HEAD>
  <TITLE>CSS - Special Offers</TITLE>
   <LINK REL=STYLESHEET TYPE=text/css HREF=corp.css>
   <LINK REL=STYLESHEET TYPE=text/css HREF=sales.css>
   <STYLE TYPE = text/css>
     H1, H2 {border-width:2; background-color:white}
     P {font-weight:bold; background-color:yellow}
     ADDRESS {text-align:center}
   </STYLE>
 </HEAD>
 <BODY>
   <H1>Corporate Swim Suits</H1>
   <H2>Special Offers</H2>
   <H3>Sec's Appeal</H3>
   <P>Itsy-bitsy, teeny-weeny, yellow polka dot bikinis..£29.99
   <H3>For the Typing Pool</H3>
   <P>Lycra one-piece with Tippex stripes.........................£34.99
   <H3>The Business Launch</H3>
   <P>Generous cut with ultra-elasticated waistband.....£19.99</P>
<ADDRESS>E-mail your order to <A HREF = mailto:sales@css.con>CSS
</A> now </ADDRESS>
</BODY>
</HTML>
```

Links **corp.css** first, then **sales.css**

Tweaks styles of **H1**, **H2**, **P** and **ADDRESS**

Background, heading font and alignment, **P** size and margins, and **ADDRESS** box effects from corp.css

Text and **ADDRESS** border colours from sales.css

Background colours, heading borders and **ADDRESS** alignment from **<STYLE>** settings

121

# Summary

❑ Style sheets allow you to redefine tags, giving fuller control over the appearance and positioning of text and images, but they can only be handled by versions 4.0 and later of the browsers.

❑ An element is a tagged section of code. Paragraphs, heading and images are block elements; items within paragraphs are inline elements.

❑ When an element is enclosed by another, they have a parent–child relationship in which style definitions in the parent element are inherited by the child.

❑ The font attributes have the same formatting options as <FONT> and other HTML styling tags, plus greater control over weight and size.

❑ The text attributes set the alignment and spacing of text.

❑ In addition to setting the colours of text, style sheets allow you to set a background colour for a paragraph, different from that of the body. Where an image is used as a body background, its repetition and position can be controlled.

❑ All block elements have margins and borders. The size and colour of these can be set to enable the accurate placing of elements.

❑ Classes and IDs allow you to have alternative styles for the same element.

❑ A style can be defined so that it only applies to an element when it is within another element, for example, how bold is displayed within a particular heading.

❑ The <DIV> and <SPAN> tags allow you to set styles within a restricted area of the page. <DIV> can also be used to position elements in (overlapping) layers in the page.

❑ Where consistent styles are required in sets of pages, external style sheets can be linked in.

# 7 Forms

Gathering feedback ............124

Text inputs ..................126

Checkboxes and radio buttons .....128

Drop-down menus ............130

Buttons ....................132

Custom buttons ..............133

Refining your form ............134

Forms for Javascript ............137

Summary ...................138

# Gathering feedback

The easiest way to get feedback from visitors to your site is just to supply an e-mail address or a **mailto:** link, but if you set up a form, you can decide exactly what sort of information you want to receive. This might be their thoughts on the content or presentation of the site, or you may want to move into the burgeoning world of e-commerce. A simple first step into this is to include in a Web page an order form which customers use to tell you what they want and where they live. The form calculates how much they have to pay (see page 159) and they send you a cheque.

## Basics

To get started, you'll need to open a form area with the **<FORM…>** tag and define two options, **ACTION** and **METHOD**, which determine how the form is dealt with. **ACTION** is a URL, either of an address (**mailto:…**), or of a program which will process the information in some way. You can find programs on the Web which perform various functions and most Internet Service Providers offer CGI scripts to process form feedback (see page 162). For now let's use a simple e-mail address:

```
<FORM ACTION=mailto:you@youraddress.com …>
```

The other option to set is **METHOD**; this takes either **POST** or **GET**. **GET** is used for things like search engines, and is a bit beyond us at the moment. Besides, HTML 4.0 deprecates this method, so it will be phased out anyway. **METHOD=POST** is what we'll use, and it just tells the browser to post the form results to the **ACTION** URL.

Inside the form, you'll need at least one kind of user **INPUT** element – text box, drop-down menu, etc. – and a **SUBMIT** button to send the form.

A very simple example of a form is shown opposite – concentrate on the way that the **<FORM>** tag is used and ignore the form's contents for the moment.

## Names and values

Every input element included in a form should have a **NAME** to identify it, so that when you get the response mailed to you, you can see which answers belong with which questions. The answers are the **VALUES** of the element, entered or selected by the user. They are returned in *name=value* pairs.

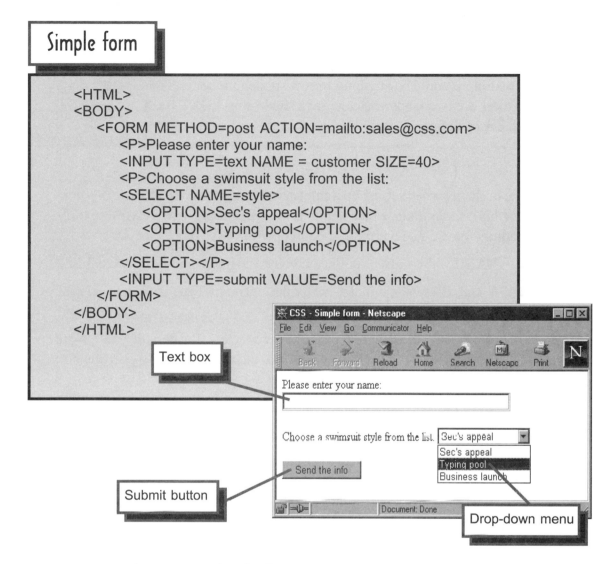

## Simple form

```
<HTML>
<BODY>
  <FORM METHOD=post ACTION=mailto:sales@css.com>
    <P>Please enter your name:
    <INPUT TYPE=text NAME = customer SIZE=40>
    <P>Choose a swimsuit style from the list:
    <SELECT NAME=style>
      <OPTION>Sec's appeal</OPTION>
      <OPTION>Typing pool</OPTION>
      <OPTION>Business launch</OPTION>
    </SELECT></P>
    <INPUT TYPE=submit VALUE=Send the info>
  </FORM>
</BODY>
</HTML>
```

Text box

Submit button

Drop-down menu

When you receive feedback, you'll probably need to save it as a text file before opening it – and when you do, you'll have a messy string of characters which needs some work to make it readable! The Replace facility of your word processor will come in handy here – and if you expect a lot of feedback, it will be worth spending time setting up a macro to tidy up the text.

Here's the feedback you might get from a simple form:

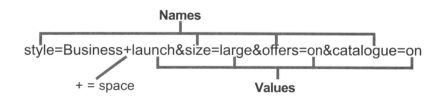

Names

style=Business+launch&size=large&offers=on&catalogue=on

+ = space

Values

# Text inputs

A text input could be anything from a single number to a mammoth essay, so there are two kinds you can use: a single-line **TEXT BOX** and a **TEXT AREA** of definable size.

## Text boxes

The basic tag when setting up a single-line text input is **<INPUT...>** – note that this is a single tag, which requires no closing tag. There are a few options that may be defined within it, though only the **NAME** is necessary:

- **NAME** – this must be defined if you are to make sense of any feedback.

- **VALUE** – sets an initial value for the text box: "Type your answer here" for instance.

- **SIZE** – sets the length of the box in characters (the default is 20). Note that users can type in more characters than this, and if they do, the box will scroll horizontally.

- **MAXLENGTH** – this limits the number of characters a user can enter.

This **<INPUT>** sets up a text box named 'slogan', with an initial and maximum size of 35 characters, and which initially displays the text 'No strapline required'.

```
<INPUT NAME=slogan SIZE=35 MAXLENGTH=35 VALUE="No strapline required">
```

## Text areas

A text area is opened with the **<TEXTAREA...>** tag, and must be closed with a **</TEXTAREA>** tag. Its size is defined in **ROWS** of text and **COLS**, where a column is one character width: the default size is 20 characters long by 2 rows deep. You cannot set an initial value for a text area, so if nothing is entered here, a blank value will be returned. A maximum length cannot be specified either – when users type in more text than there is room to display, vertical scroll bars allow them to view it all. As always, you will need to define a **NAME** for the element to identify it:

```
<TEXTAREA NAME=comments COLS=60 ROWS=4></TEXTAREA>
```

```
<HTML>
<HEAD>
    <TITLE>CSS - Simple form</TITLE>
</HEAD>
<BODY>
    <FORM METHOD=post ACTION=mailto:sales@css.com>
        <P>Please enter your company name:
        <INPUT NAME=username>
        <P>Strapline/motto (maximum 6 words):
        <INPUT NAME=slogan SIZE=35 MAXLENGTH=35
            VALUE="No strapline required">
        <P>Any specific design requirements? Please detail below:<BR>
        <TEXTAREA NAME=design_comments COLS=50 ROWS=5>
        </TEXTAREA>
        <P><INPUT TYPE=submit>
    </FORM>
</BODY>
</HTML>
```

A simple text input

Default value to return if user types nothing

A text area

Submit button – see p.132

Give prompts so that people know what they're supposed to be entering

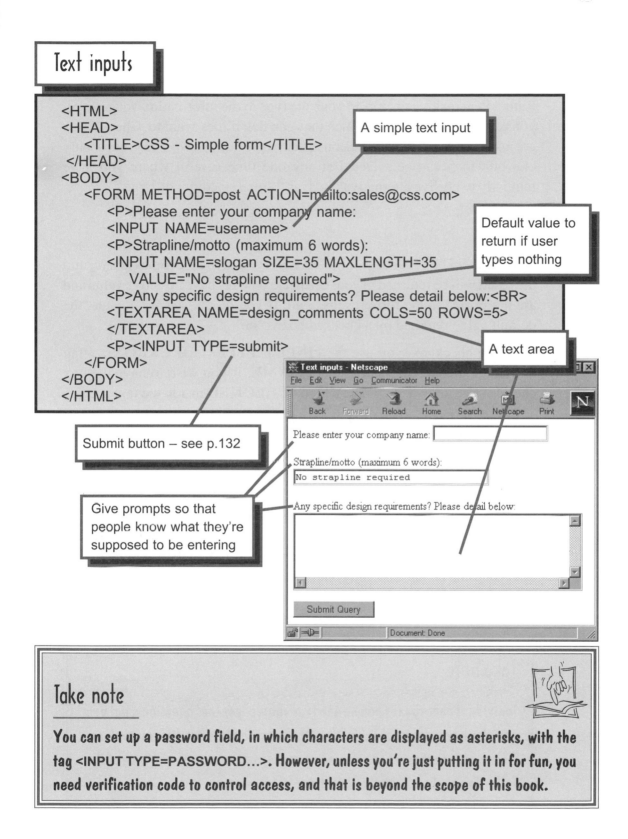

## Take note

You can set up a password field, in which characters are displayed as asterisks, with the tag <INPUT TYPE=PASSWORD...>. However, unless you're just putting it in for fun, you need verification code to control access, and that is beyond the scope of this book.

# Checkboxes and radio buttons

Rather than making visitors to your site type in the information you require, you can give them choices which they can tick if they want to. Checkboxes are just boxes which users click on to tick; radio buttons work in groups, only one of which can be selected at any one time (useful where you have mutually exclusive alternatives such as "Small, medium or large?")

## Checkboxes

When a checkbox is checked, the **VALUE** you give it becomes active, and the result will be returned to you. Unchecked boxes have no active value and are not posted in the form results at all. If you do not specify a value, the default value returned by a checked box is 'on'.

To add a checkbox, you use the **<INPUT TYPE=CHECKBOX...>** tag (without a closing tag) and give it a **NAME**. If you wish to have the box checked already when it appears, type **CHECKED** inside the tag:

```
<INPUT TYPE=CHECKBOX NAME=junk_mail
    VALUE=please_send CHECKED>
```

## Radio buttons

A radio button is added to a page with the **<INPUT TYPE=RADIO...>** tag. A group of radio buttons is defined by adding more than one radio button and assigning all of them the same **NAME**. You then assign different **VALUES** to each so that choice is clear in the returned form. As only one radio button in a group can be selected, only one *name=value* pair will be returned to you from the group; all unselected buttons have inactive values and are ignored.

## Take note

Individual checkboxes can be used for simple 'yes/no' questions, but you can also have several checkboxes with the same name but different values. This means that users can choose more than one answer to a 'Which of the following apply...?' kind of question.

# Checkboxes and radio buttons

```
<HTML>
<HEAD>
    <TITLE>Checkboxes and radio buttons</TITLE>
</HEAD>
<BODY>
    <FORM METHOD=post ACTION=mailto:sales@css.com>
        <P>Tick the extra features you require:<BR>
        <INPUT TYPE=CHECKBOX NAME=extras VALUE=goggles>
            Matching goggles<BR>
        <INPUT TYPE=CHECKBOX NAME=extras VALUE=flippers>
            Matching flippers<BR>
        <INPUT TYPE=CHECKBOX NAME=extras VALUE=ring>
            Matching rubber ring

        <P>Please choose a size:
        <INPUT TYPE=RADIO NAME=size
            VALUE=small> Tea boy
        <INPUT TYPE=RADIO NAME=size VALUE=medium>
        Middleweight management
        <INPUT TYPE=RADIO NAME=size VALUE=large>Fat cat
        <P>Tick here to order our winter catalogue:
        <INPUT TYPE=CHECKBOX NAME=catalogue CHECKED>
        <P><INPUT TYPE=SUBMIT VALUE="Send the info">
    </FORM>
</BODY>
</HTML>
```

> Users can submit more than one item under the heading **extras**

> Only one of these three options can be selected

> Be sneaky and nudge users towards the answer you want to hear...

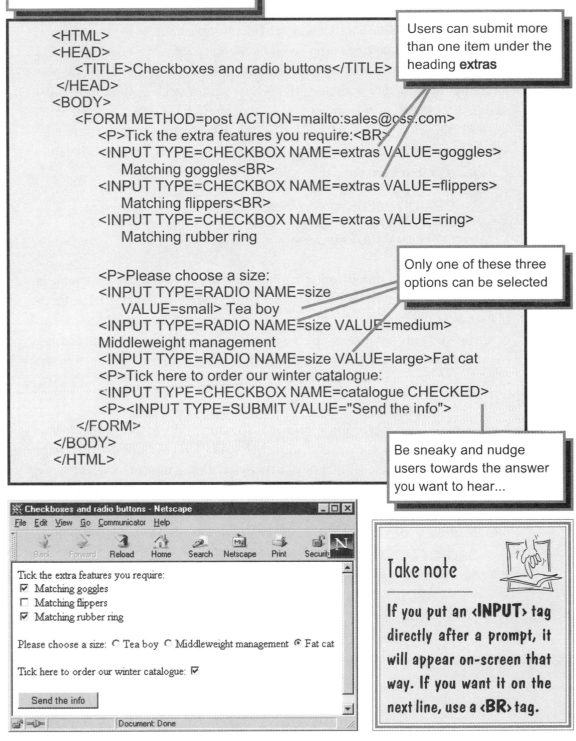

**Checkboxes and radio buttons - Netscape**

File  Edit  View  Go  Communicator  Help

Back  Forward  Reload  Home  Search  Netscape  Print  Security

Tick the extra features you require:
☑ Matching goggles
☐ Matching flippers
☑ Matching rubber ring

Please choose a size:  ○ Tea boy  ○ Middleweight management  ● Fat cat

Tick here to order our winter catalogue: ☑

Send the info

Document: Done

## Take note

If you put an **‹INPUT›** tag directly after a prompt, it will appear on-screen that way. If you want it on the next line, use a **‹BR›** tag.

**129**

# Drop-down menus

Drop-down menus are another way to offer multiple choices to your visitors, but with the advantage of being economical on space. Two tags are needed to put a drop-down menu on your form: a **<SELECT>...</SELECT>** pair to create the structure and an **<OPTION>** tag for each option. You must assign a **NAME** to the menu inside the **<SELECT...>** tag; and each **<OPTION...>** needs a **VALUE** for feedback and some text to describe the option in the menu. A simple menu of three colours could be made like this:

```
Pick a colour from the list:
<SELECT NAME=colour>
    <OPTION VALUE=green>Sea green
    <OPTION VALUE=blue>Sky blue
    <OPTION VALUE=brown>Mud brown
</SELECT>
```

By default, browsers will only display the first option until the menu is opened, but you can override this by setting the **SIZE** in the **<SELECT...>** tag – this is the number of options initially displayed. You might decide to do this if you only have a few options and there's room on the form to display them all, but it becomes more useful when dealing with multiple selections.

## Multiple selections

Normally only one selection is allowed, so you will have one *name=value* pair returned to you, but you can allow **MULTIPLE** selections if you wish. Users can then use the [Shift] or [Ctrl] keys with the mouse to select more than one option. When multiple selections are allowed, browsers usually display several options rather than just one, so you may want to specify the number of options visible (scroll bars will allow users access to the others):

```
<SELECT MULTIPLE SIZE=5>
```

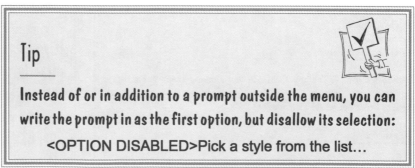

### Tip

**Instead of or in addition to a prompt outside the menu, you can write the prompt in as the first option, but disallow its selection:**

```
<OPTION DISABLED>Pick a style from the list...
```

```
<HTML>
<HEAD>
 <TITLE>CSS - Drop-down menus</TITLE>
</HEAD>
<BODY>
   <FORM METHOD=post ACTION=mailto:sales@css.com>

   <P>Pick a style:<BR>
   <SELECT>
      <OPTION DISABLED>Please choose a style from the list...
      <OPTION VALUE=surf>Radical surf shorts
      <OPTION VALUE=poseur>Padded posing pouch (leopardskin
         only)
      <OPTION VALUE=bikini>Bikini
      <OPTION VALUE=vic>Victorian style evening swimsuit with
      bustle (for the elegant pool party)
   </SELECT>
   <P>Pick a colour (choose more than one colour for stripy
      swimsuits):<BR>
   <SELECT MULTIPLE SIZE=4>
      <OPTION VALUE=lemon>Lemon yellow
      <OPTION VALUE=lime>Lime green
      <OPTION VALUE=rasp>Raspberry red
      <OPTION VALUE=orange>Orange orange
   </SELECT>
   <P><INPUT TYPE=SUBMIT>
</FORM>
</BODY>
</HTML>
```

Prevent selection of this option – it's used as a prompt

Keep **values** simple and clear

**MULTIPLE** lets users select several options

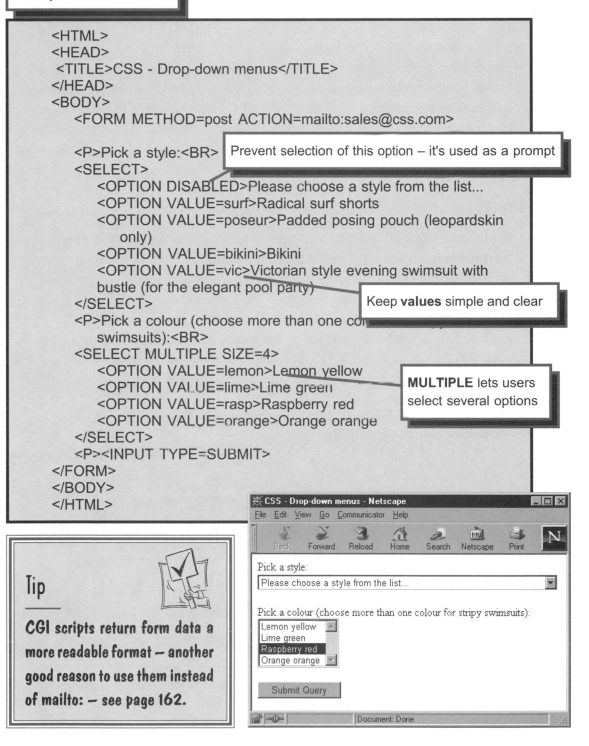

**Tip**

CGI scripts return form data a more readable format – another good reason to use them instead of mailto: – see page 162.

Netscape window:
CSS - Drop-down menus - Netscape
File  Edit  View  Go  Communicator  Help
Back  Forward  Reload  Home  Search  Netscape  Print

Pick a style:
Please choose a style from the list...

Pick a colour (choose more than one colour for stripy swimsuits):
Lemon yellow
Lime green
Raspberry red
Orange orange

Submit Query

Document: Done

# Buttons

Every form must have at least one button – a **SUBMIT** button to send the information to you – and most will also have a **RESET** button to clear responses entered by users, in case they change their mind. You can also create custom buttons, which will run scripts to perform other functions. All of these can be created using either an **<INPUT...>** or **<BUTTON...>** tags, both of which have pretty much the same effect. The former is simpler to use, but the latter offers more features, such as being able to use an image to decorate a button.

## Submit and reset

Whichever tags you use, you will need to specify **TYPE= submit**, **reset** or **button** (to run a script). The **VALUE** of a button is the text which appears on it, and is submitted along with a **NAME** if you have specified one – you may have more than one submit button on a form and might use this to glean some further information about your user. In the case of the **<INPUT...>** tag, the text is explicitly defined as the button's **VALUE**; when using the **<BUTTON...>** tags, the **VALUE** is the text between the tags:

```
<INPUT TYPE=submit NAME=valuedClient VALUE="Send by
   1st class email">
<BUTTON TYPE=submit NAME=cheapskate>Send by budget
   carrier pigeon</BUTTON>
<INPUT TYPE=reset VALUE="Whoops! I made a mistake!">
```

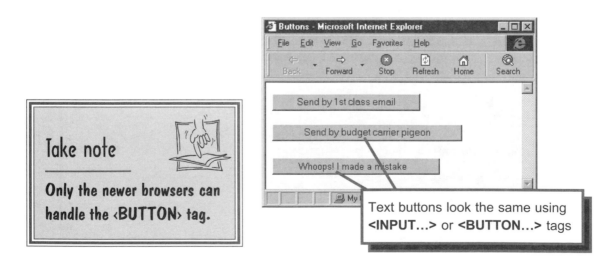

**Take note**

**Only the newer browsers can handle the ‹BUTTON› tag.**

Text buttons look the same using **<INPUT...>** or **<BUTTON...>** tags

# Custom buttons

There is an **INPUT TYPE** designed specifically to create an image which is used as a submit button. With this, you specify an image file as the button's **SRC** instead of typing in a text **VALUE**:

```
<INPUT TYPE=image SRC=images/submit.gif>
```

You cannot use images with the **<INPUT...>** tag for other kinds of button. If you want an image on a reset or other button, put an **<IMG SRC...>** tag instead of text between the **<BUTTON...>** tags:

```
<BUTTON TYPE=button onClick="totalCost()"> <IMG SRC=
    images/abacus.gif> </BUTTON>
```

This one uses **onClick** to run a JavaScript function. See page 155 to find out more about these.

Since the buttons on a form are fairly crucial to it working, you should define a text alternative to your images in case your visitor cannot view them:

```
<IMG SRC="send.gif" ALT="Submit">
```

You might also like to put both text and images on a button:

```
<BUTTON TYPE="reset"><IMG SRC="images/doh.gif">
    Clear the form!</BUTTON>
```

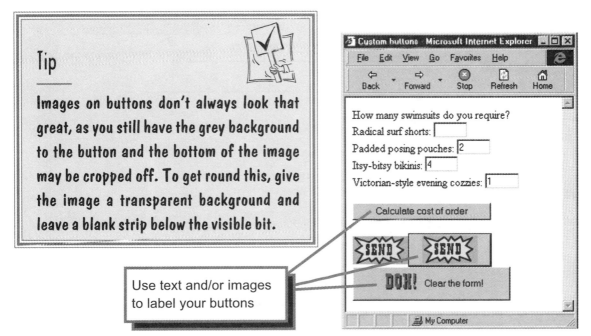

## Tip

Images on buttons don't always look that great, as you still have the grey background to the button and the bottom of the image may be cropped off. To get round this, give the image a transparent background and leave a blank strip below the visible bit.

Use text and/or images to label your buttons

# Refining your form

You now know how to create all the elements you may need on a form, and you can lay them out using style sheets or tables, but there are a couple of features which can further refine your form's appearance and functionality. **FIELDSET**s group form elements together – if you have a lengthy form, you can break it up into sections: personal information, order form, feedback, etc., while **LABEL**s link an input element to its prompt. Both are very useful to speech-based browsers for the visually impaired, as they clearly identify what information is required in each section and at each input.

## Fieldsets

To group elements into a fieldset, put a **<FIELDSET>** tag before the first and **</FIELDSET>** after the last. To identify a fieldset, add a **<LEGEND>**, which can be aligned to the **top**, **left**, **right**, or **bottom** of the fieldset.

```
<FIELDSET>
<LEGEND ALIGN="top">Delivery information</LEGEND>
  … form elements, prompts, layout code, etc. …
</FIELDSET>
```

Legend

The form is broken into manageable chunks using fieldsets

# Labels

When you place a prompt for a form element next to it, you visually associate the two and know what information is required for it. Speech-based browsers, on the other hand, will probably not be able to make the same intuitive leap, and will need things spelled out clearly for them.

If your prompt and form element are right next to each other (not separated by table cells, for instance), then you can simply enclose both in **<LABEL>...</LABEL>** tags:

```
<LABEL>Enter your name: <INPUT NAME=user_name></LABEL>
```

However, if you are using some other method to lay out your form clearly, you will need to create an association for each element and its label. This is done by assigning the element an **ID** to identify it, and then referring to this inside the **<LABEL...>** tag using the **FOR=** option (in practice, you'll probably find that the label precedes the input element, but that's OK):

```
<TD><LABEL FOR=largeSize>Fat Cat Trunks</LABEL></TD>
<TD><INPUT TYPE=radio NAME=size VALUE=large
    ID=largeSize></TD>
```

This second approach has the advantage of associating the two tags so that clicking on the label is the same as clicking on the input.

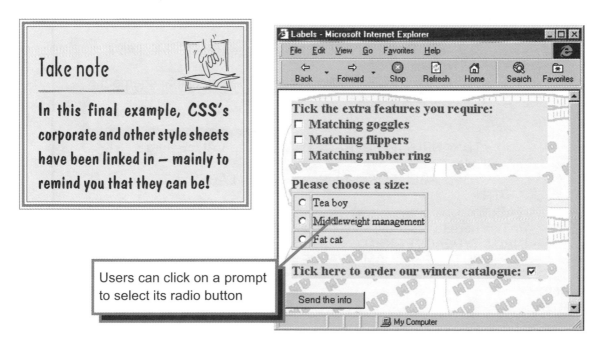

## Take note

In this final example, CSS's corporate and other style sheets have been linked in – mainly to remind you that they can be!

Users can click on a prompt to select its radio button

135

```
<HTML>
<HEAD>
   <TITLE>Labels</TITLE>
   <LINK REL=STYLESHEET TYPE=text/css HREF=corp.css>
   <LINK REL=STYLESHEET TYPE=text/css HREF=sales.css>
   <STYLE TYPE = text/css>
      P {font-weight:bold; background-color:yellow}
   </STYLE>
</HEAD>
<BODY>
   <FORM METHOD=post ACTION=mailto:sales@css.com>
      <P>Tick the extra features you require:<BR>
      <LABEL><INPUT TYPE=CHECKBOX NAME=extras VALUE=goggles>
         Matching goggles</LABEL><BR>
      <LABEL><INPUT TYPE=CHECKBOX NAME=extras VALUE=flippers>
         Matching flippers</LABEL><BR>
      <LABEL><INPUT TYPE=CHECKBOX NAME=extras VALUE=ring>
         Matching rubber ring</LABEL><BR>
      <P>Please choose a size:
      <TABLE BORDER=1>
         <TR>
            <TD><INPUT TYPE=RADIO NAME=size VALUE=small
               ID=smallSize></TD>
            <TD><LABEL FOR=smallSize>Tea boy</LABEL></TD>
         </TR>
         <TR>
            <TD><INPUT TYPE=RADIO NAME=size VALUE=medium
               ID=mediumSize>
            <TD><LABEL FOR=mediumSize>Middleweight management
               </LABEL></TD>
         </TR>
         <TR>
            <TD><INPUT TYPE=RADIO NAME=size VALUE=large
            ID=largeSize>
            <TD><LABEL FOR=largeSize>Fat cat</LABEL></TD>
         </TR>
      </TABLE>
      <P>Tick here to order our winter catalogue:
      <INPUT TYPE=CHECKBOX NAME=catalogue CHECKED>
      </P><INPUT TYPE=SUBMIT VALUE="Send the info">
   </FORM>
</BODY>
</HTML>
```

Corporate and sales style sheets linked to the page

Use the prompt as a label

Labels linked through ID option

136

# Forms for Javascript

To use the Javascript command **onClick**, which is a very useful one, you either need a link or a button. More often than not, a link is rather unhelpful, because you don't want to send your visitor anywhere! In these cases, you need a button – but buttons can only exist within forms, so you have to define an 'empty' form (with no actual inputs) around the button. As with other buttons, the **VALUE** is the text which appears on it; remember to set this, or you will end up with a tiny little grey rectangle for a button.

## Forms for buttons

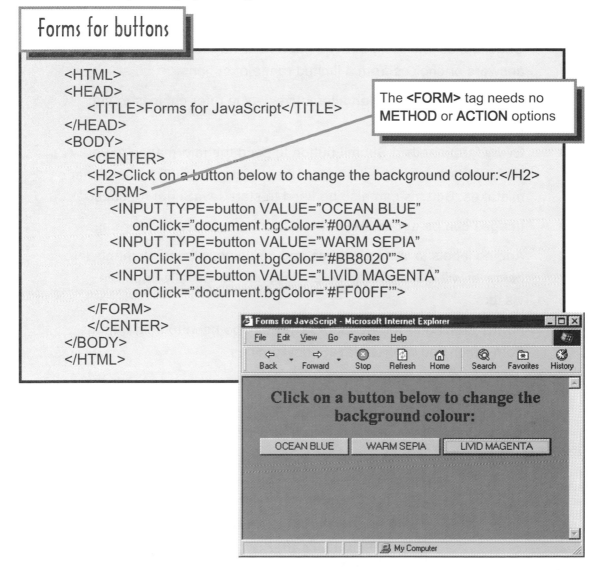

```
<HTML>
<HEAD>
   <TITLE>Forms for JavaScript</TITLE>
</HEAD>
<BODY>
   <CENTER>
   <H2>Click on a button below to change the background colour:</H2>
   <FORM>
      <INPUT TYPE=button VALUE="OCEAN BLUE"
         onClick="document.bgColor='#00AAAA'">
      <INPUT TYPE=button VALUE="WARM SEPIA"
         onClick="document.bgColor='#BB8020'">
      <INPUT TYPE=button VALUE="LIVID MAGENTA"
         onClick="document.bgColor='#FF00FF'">
   </FORM>
   </CENTER>
</BODY>
</HTML>
```

The **<FORM>** tag needs no **METHOD** or **ACTION** options

Forms for JavaScript – Microsoft Internet Explorer

File   Edit   View   Go   Favorites   Help

Back   Forward   Stop   Refresh   Home   Search   Favorites   History

**Click on a button below to change the background colour:**

OCEAN BLUE   WARM SEPIA   LIVID MAGENTA

My Computer

# Summary

- ❏ Forms offer the simplest and usually the most convenient way to gather feedback from your visitors.

- ❏ Each input element should be accompanied by a prompt so that visitors know what is required. Elements must be named so that the values they return can be identified.

- ❏ Text can be collected in one-line INPUT boxes or multi-line TEXTAREAs.

- ❏ Checkboxes and radio buttons are a neat way to collect yes/no answers or choices from a limited range of options.

- ❏ Drop-down menus are an alternative way to offer choices to your visitors.

- ❏ Every form needs a Submit button to send the information to you. A Reset button will let visitors clear their information if they have made mistakes. Buttons can also be used to start JavaScript routines.

- ❏ Images can be turned into buttons for more variety on your page.

- ❏ Adding labels to input elements and grouping relating elements into fieldsets will make a form more accessible to visually-impaired visitors.

- ❏ Forms aren't only for feedback. They can be used to hold buttons from which you can run JavaScript routines.

## Tip

If you are expecting to receive quite a few completed forms, you may want to set up a new e-mail address to receive them — most ISPs offer several addresses per account.

# 8 Sound and animation

Putting sound on the page . . . . . . . 140

Recording sound . . . . . . . . . . . . . . . 142

RealAudio . . . . . . . . . . . . . . . . . . 144

Video clips . . . . . . . . . . . . . . . . . . 145

Animations . . . . . . . . . . . . . . . . . . 146

Flash and Shockwave . . . . . . . . . . . 148

Marquees . . . . . . . . . . . . . . . . . . . 149

Summary . . . . . . . . . . . . . . . . . . . 150

# Putting sound on the page

There are two approaches to this: embed the sound file in the 'background' so that it plays when the page is opened, or have a clickable link to it. Background sounds should be in formats that can normally be handled by browsers, such as **.wav** or **MIDI**, otherwise your visitors may wait for a file to download, only to hear nothing. Linked files can be in any format as visitors can ignore them if they do not have a suitable player.

There are three ways to set up background sounds.

```
<EMBED SRC=missy.wav HIDDEN = true AUTOSTART = true
LOOP = true>
or  <EMBED SRC = audio.mid WIDTH = 145>

<BGSOUND SRC=audio.mid LOOP=infinite>
```

The first type of **<EMBED …>** sets a sound file running permanently in the background. It hides the audio player, starts it as soon as the file is loaded, and loops round to play it again and again until the visitor leaves the page.

In the second **<EMBED…>** the audio controls are visible – and they need a **WIDTH** of about 145 pixels to display properly. The **AUTOSTART** and **LOOP** options can still be used, but serve less purpose as visitors can turn the sound on and off for themselves.

**<EMBED…>** will work in both Netscape and in newer versions of Explorer. If you want sounds to be heard by earlier versions of Explorer, you must use **<BGSOUND…>**. Its **LOOP** option is more variable, allowing you to set the number of times the clip is played ('infinite' keeps playing over and over until the user leaves the page or clicks the **Stop loading** button).

In theory, you could include both **<EMBED…>** and **<BGSOUND…>** lines to cater for all browsers, but with **AUTOSTART** set to true the newer versions of Explorer would then play the clip twice, overlapping – and it would sound horrendous!

If you include your sound as a link to the file you avoid browser confusion, and can give visitors information about the file size and type before they try to download it. To do this, you just provide a normal **<A HREF…>** link to the file and leave the rest to your visitors (and if you're using RealAudio or mp3, it would be nice to also provide links to the suppliers of the playback programs – read about these formats on pages 142–44 for more details).

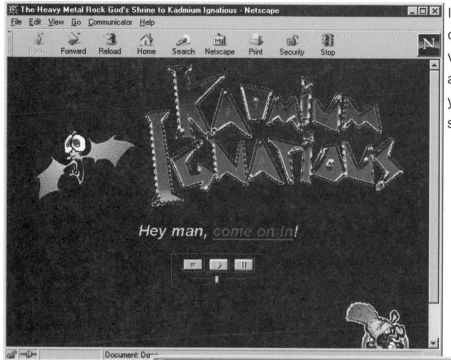

If the playback controls are visible, they appear wherever you embed the sound file

A link makes visitors' lives much easier - you can give them an informed choice rather than force-feeding them sounds

**141**

# Recording sound

Sound for the Web can be saved in several formats, all of which have their advantages and disadvantages that make them suitable for different uses. **.wav** and **mp3** files are for high-quality recordings of voice and music, but are large – particularly **.wav** files – and must be downloaded completely before they can be heard. **MIDI** files are nice and small, but only transmit synthesiser music, not any kind of recording. **RealAudio** files are encoded recordings, including voice, music and even video; the files are small and can be heard as they download, but interference or delays to your Internet connection may affect the quality.

## MIDI and mp3 files

If you have a synthesiser you may be making your own **MIDI** tracks, but if not, you can download files from the web and then use them on your site (taking care over the copyright, of course). Try the *Soundstore* at **http://www.soundstore.com/home.html** to see what sort of stuff is around.

**mp3** is a new protocol which compresses CD-quality sound into relatively small files – a couple of Mb per track, rather than the 15Mb or so a .wav file would use. There is software available for producing mp3 files – do a search for 'mp3 tools'. For audio CD to mp3 conversion you need a 'ripper' to turn the CD into a wav file, then an 'encoder' to convert this to mp3.

## .wav files from Sound Recorder

Unless you have some special sound software (which should have its own instructions), use the Windows **Sound recorder** to record audio files. You'll find it under **Programs**, **Accessories**, **Multimedia** on the **Start** menu. Here's how to use it to record sound from a CD.

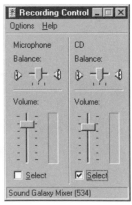

1   Open Sound Recorder and choose **New...** from the **File** menu.

2   Open the **Edit** menu and select **Audio Properties**. Select **Adjust volume for Recording** and at the **Recording Control** panel, select the **CD**.

**3** Click the red record button to begin and set your CD going at the point you want to start recording. Don't worry about beginning too early or ending too late, because you can cut the beginning and end later. Position the slider at a point where you want to start or stop, open the **Edit** menu and choose **Delete Before** or **After Current Position**.

Edit and add effects

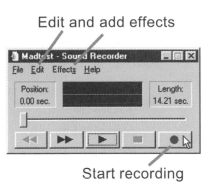

Start recording

You can also play with the **Effects** to speed up or slow down the sample, add an echo or reverse it (for the Satanists among you).

When you have your clip, save it and open **File… Properties**. Click **Convert now…** to see if you can reduce the file size without losing too much sound quality – you'll see that even a few seconds of music takes up a huge amount of space.

This 14 second clip is nearly 1.3Mb at CD quality

Convert the file to a lower-quality recording

Experiment with quality levels from the drop-down menu to find a suitable one

**143**

# RealAudio

To create or listen to RealAudio files, you need software from **RealNetworks** (www.real.com); the sophisticated recording and editing facilities have to be bought, but you can download a basic version (*RealProducer*) for free.

Record a clip as a .wav file using Sound recorder, edit it as necessary, then use RealProducer to convert it to a RealAudio (**.rm** or **.ram**) file – you can convert video files into RealVideo streams in the same way. It's fairly simple and there are wizards to guide you through the process. If your ISP has RealAudio server software, you can set up your files to play according to the capacity of the user's modem, or 'stream' it (play as it downloads). If they don't you have to choose a transmission speed and only transmit at that rate.

Convert an existing file, record a new one from CD player or video camera, or produce a live broadcast

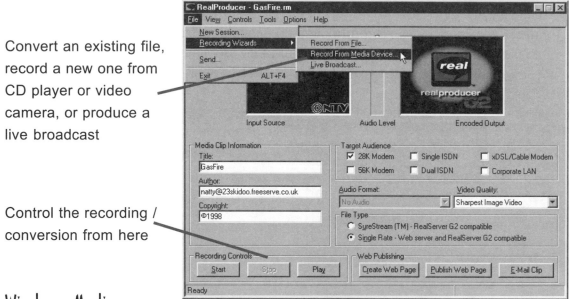

Control the recording / conversion from here

## Windows Media

Windows Media is an alternative to RealAudio – it does much the same sort of thing, and once again there are free tools for converting .wav files and .mp3s to Windows Media format. Get the tools and the Player from **www.microsoft.com/windows/windowsmedia**. The conversion software is easy to use, and there are lots of tutorials and samples at the developer's center – www.microsoft.com/windows/windowsmedia/en/developers.

Windows Media Player handles most kinds of image, audio and video – but not RealAudio or RealVideo.

# Video clips

If you've tried downloading a movie clip from the Web, you'll know that it's a slow business, so don't expect people to sit and wait for your video-from-the-top-of-the-sightseeing-bus to come in! If you've got a good one, though, here's how to do it. Basically it's very simple – you save the video file (**video.avi** or **video.mpg**) on your server and then just provide a link to it from your page:

    Have a look at <A HREF=images/badday.mpg>this</A>!

It's worth putting a note by the link warning potential viewers of the file size, so that they can decide whether or not they've got time to download it then. When the file is downloaded, the browser should spawn a suitable plug-in to watch it with, or viewers may have to open it themselves.

Alternatively, you could replace the **.avi** or **.mpg** with a compressed version of it. Use WinZip to compress the file, save it as before and make sure that the link points to the **.zip** file (you may then want to explain to your viewers that they'll need to unzip it to view it).

A still from a 'computer-rage' incident supposedly caught on a security camera - have a look at http://sites.inka.de/~sleipnir/badday/index.html (or if that page has disappeared, try finding badday.mpg through a search engine – there are enough versions around!)

## Take note

If you use RealAudio or RealVideo files on your site, have a link to the RealNetworks site so that visitors can pick up RealPlayer if they need it. Newer versions of RealPlayer will display most kinds of audio, video and static images, even Flash files, but not streaming Windows Media.

# Animations

You can liven up your pages without huge sound or video files by using a few nice animated GIFs – but beware of overdoing it, as too many can easily be distracting! Animated GIFs are inserted on a page in exactly the same way as normal images, but you will need a piece of animation software to create them. Microsoft's GIF Animator is quite small and simple to use, and Jasc's Animation Shop, which comes with Paint Shop Pro 5, has a sophisticated range of extra features which make it a lot of fun. It's also easier to take ready-made animations and alter them in Animation Shop, as you have the usual Paint Shop Pro drawing tools at hand to touch up individual frames – in GIF Animator, you will have to copy and paste the frames from the animator to an image editor and back.

## Cartoon animation

For most animated GIFs you will need to create several distinct images, which the animation program will put together as frames of the animation. Bear in mind that the more images you have in your animation, the larger the file will be, so you have the familiar trade-off between quality and speed of download. To keep file sizes small, try to avoid replacing the whole image when much of it remains stationary – if you have a little man waving his arm, for instance, you will ideally have one initial image of the whole man and then several smaller images of his arm, which will need to be aligned correctly in the subsequent frames if they are to work. GIF Animator is good for this, as you can specify exactly whereabouts in the frame the next image is to fit. Animation Shop just gives you the choice of aligning it centrally or with the top left corner.

In the example opposite, a rock singer bangs his head back and forth. An initial image shows the whole figure, while subsequent images of the moving head start from the same top left corner, but have the unchanged body cropped off. If you do this, you will have to make sure that the initial image is not wiped off before the next is displayed – in GIF Animator, you will need to set the **Undraw** method to **Leave**. Probably the best way to get to grips with animated GIFs is to search the Web for a few good ones, open them in an animation package and see how they were put together. There are dozens of good sites which offer free examples (usually for home use only) – search for 'free animated GIFs' in any search engine and you'll find some.

Cut out and copy the portion of the image which is to move

Crop the original image to cover only the changed area and delete the part which will move

Paste the cutout into the cropped image and rotate it

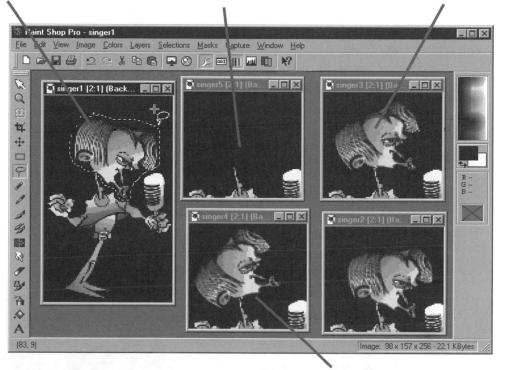

Repeat, increasing the rotation, for subsequent frames

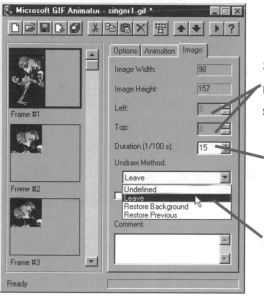

Set the number of pixels from the margins of the frame that a smaller image is to be displayed

Set the length of time a frame is to be displayed for

Set the **Undraw** method to **Leave** to stop frames being wiped off the screen before the next is displayed

# Flash and Shockwave

Flash allows you to create lovely smooth (and fast-downloading) animations, and integrate sounds and interactivity. Shockwave is a turbo-charged version which is often used for creating games for online use. You've probably come across Web pages which use these packages before – you need the players to run them, so if you don't already have them installed you'll usually be offered a link to the Macromedia download page (**www.macromedia.com/downloads**).

If you're interested in producing Flash or Shockwave web pages, you'll need to buy the software. It's not cheap and a little daunting to begin with, but it's a very powerful package. If you have the time to learn how to use it, and you're serious about producing top quality web pages, it may be worth investing in. If you've got this far through this book without too much difficulty, then Flash certainly won't be beyond you!

There are some great Flash animations at **www.sparkisland.com**

# Marquees

Only Explorer has Marquees. These slide back and forth across the page, and are a simple way to get movement without building animations from scratch. Write the material to be animated in **<MARQUEE...> </MARQUEE>** tags, setting these options as you wish:

- **BEHAVIOR** – can be set to **scroll**, which makes text appear letter by letter on one side of the screen and scrolls it across and off to the other side; the process then repeats. **Slide** does much the same, but the whole message disappears when the first letter reaches the other side. **Alternate** makes text bounce from side to side.

- **DIRECTION** – either **left** (right to left), the default, or **right** (left to right).

- **SCROLLAMOUNT** – the number of pixels which it moves each step.

- **SCROLLDELAY** – the time in milliseconds between each step. The default settings are 6 pixels and 90 milliseconds.

Text in a marquee can be formatted as normal, and line breaks, tables and images freely added – though some things can confuse the browser; setting an image's **ALIGNMENT** to **left** or **right**, for instance.

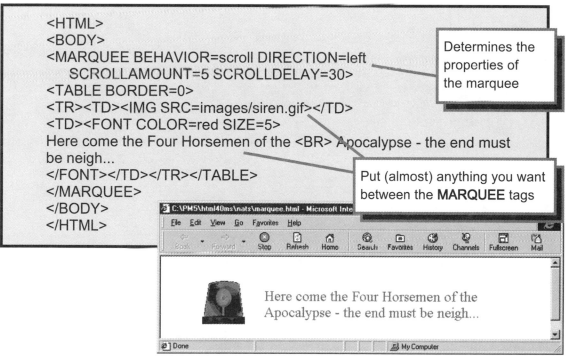

```
<HTML>
<BODY>
<MARQUEE BEHAVIOR=scroll DIRECTION=left
    SCROLLAMOUNT=5 SCROLLDELAY=30>
<TABLE BORDER=0>
<TR><TD><IMG SRC=images/siren.gif></TD>
<TD><FONT COLOR=red SIZE=5>
Here come the Four Horsemen of the <BR> Apocalypse - the end must
be neigh...
</FONT></TD></TR></TABLE>
</MARQUEE>
</BODY>
</HTML>
```

Determines the properties of the marquee

Put (almost) anything you want between the **MARQUEE** tags

C:\PM5\html40ms\nats\marquee.html - Microsoft Inte

File   Edit   View   Go   Favorites   Help

Back   Forward   Stop   Refresh   Home   Search   Favorites   History   Channels   Fullscreen   Mail

Here come the Four Horsemen of the Apocalypse - the end must be neigh...

Done                                    My Computer

# Summary

❑    Sound clips can be embedded into a page, and can play automatically – and continuously – if desired. The player controls can be hidden away, or left visible for the visitors' use.

❑    Sound Recorder can be used to create your own sound files, capturing material from CD or through the microphone.

❑    With RealAudio, you can have 'streaming' sound, which visitors can hear immediately, instead of having to wait for files to download.

❑    Video clips can be added to pages, but it must be remembered that even short clips need large files.

❑    Animated GIFs can enliven a page. You need suitable software – and a bit of artistic flair – to create them, but there are plenty of ready-made examples freely available on the Internet.

❑    Internet Explorer can display animated text produced by the <MARQUEE> tag.

# 9 Active pages

Programming languages . . . . . . . . . 152

JavaScript . . . . . . . . . . . . . . . . . . . 153

Working with objects . . . . . . . . . . . 155

The Status line . . . . . . . . . . . . . . . . 157

Feedback on-line . . . . . . . . . . . . . . 159

CGI . . . . . . . . . . . . . . . . . . . . . . . . 162

Java applets . . . . . . . . . . . . . . . . . 164

Summary . . . . . . . . . . . . . . . . . . . . 168

# Programming languages

Sounds and animated GIFs will add activity to a page, but if you want interactivity, you must turn to the programming languages. There are a number of these, of which the key ones are:

● JavaScript is the simplest to learn and to write, and gives a good level of interactivity for minimal effort. Its code is written directly into the HTML document and interpreted and executed line-by-line as it is read by the browser. The code may be a single statement to perform one simple task, or a multi-line program. Because it is interpreted, JavaScript code run relatively slowly, but as the code only adds text to the page, it adds little to the download time.

● Java is a full-blown programming language based on C++. It takes time to master, but can be used to create highly interactive games, site navigation systems and other programs. Java applets (programs in Web pages) are compiled (converted from human-readable text into code for the machine) and saved as separate files, which must be downloaded before they can be run. As even the smallest Java applet will be at least 30Kb – and they can be much larger – their use adds a significant downloading overhead to pages. This time cost should be balanced out by the fact that Java applets run much faster than JavaScript code. There isn't room in this book to teach you Java, but we'll look at how to incorporate ready-made applets into your pages.

● CGI (Common Gateway Interface) is not a language, but a standard way of setting up programs to run on servers. There's no point in learning about CGI unless you are in an organisation that has its own server, or your ISP is happy to let you load up and run CGI scripts on their machine. However, most ISPs do have a bank of CGI scripts which you can call on, from your Web pages, to perform certain tasks. Hit counters and feedback from forms are common uses of CGI – see page 162.

● XML (eXtensible Markup Language) is the newest language for the Web, but looks set to become increasingly important in the near future. Amongst other things, it allows you to structure data and interrogate it directly within Web pages. Its main use is probably going to be in those organisations that have large product or information databases that they want to make easily accessible over the Web.

# JavaScript

JavaScript is an object-oriented language – don't worry, I'm not going to let you get bogged down in the theory of programming – which for practical purposes means this: it knows about the kind of objects that are found on the screen and on Web pages – the status line, the page background, images, boxes and buttons on forms, and the like. It knows what their properties are and is aware of events that happen to them. This means that you can use JavaScript to respond to the click of a button or the mouse's movement, and that response can be to change the properties of an object – write a message in the status bar, change the page colour, open a new window or whatever.

JavaScript code can be written into your pages – and run from them – in several ways. All three are shown in use in the example on the next page.

## <SCRIPT>

The simplest method is to enclose the code in **<SCRIPT>...</SCRIPT>** tags in the **BODY** area of a document.

```
<SCRIPT>
    alert("Hello")
</SCRIPT>
```

The quotes are essential in JavaScript

When the page is opened, the code is executed as soon as it is downloaded. This is fine for short and simple scripts, but if the script refers to an object further down on the page, you have problems – if that part of the page has not been downloaded when the code tries to access it, the script will crash.

## Attached code

JavaScript code can be attached directly to the event handler of an HTML object, and will be executed when the event occurs.

<INPUT TYPE = button VALUE = Hi onClick = "alert('Have a nice day')">

In this case, the event is a click on the button, and the code will display an **Alert** message box.

## Functions

Scripts can be written into the **<HEAD>** area. Individual lines of code will be executed as soon as they are loaded, but the code can also be written into *functions* – self-contained blocks of code.

```
<SCRIPT>
function howdo()
{
    alert("How are you?")
}
</SCRIPT>
```

The function by itself does nothing. It will be executed when it is called from a line of JavaScript in a **<SCRIPT>** block, or attached to an object, somewhere in the **<BODY>** part of the document.

The (brackets) at the end of the **function...** line are essential, and can be used to transfer information between the function and the rest of the code.

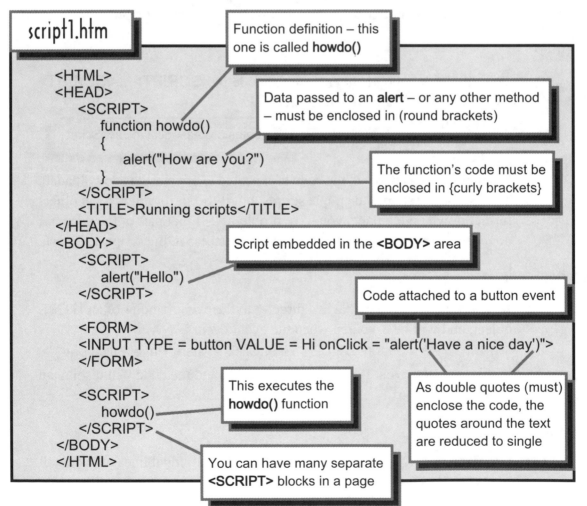

# Working with objects

## Events

The computer's operating system constantly scans the screen, keyboard, mouse, modem and other peripherals for incoming information and passes relevant inputs to JavaScript 'event handlers'. By writing event handlers into your code, you can make it respond to the users – and to other activities. There are a dozen event handlers, including these which we'll be using later.

- **onClick** applies to buttons, checkboxes and selection elements on forms. It is activated by a click of the left mouse button.

- **onFocus** applies to all screen objects and is activated when one comes 'into focus'. For a window, this means when it is opened; for a form element, it means initially the topmost, then others as they are selected.

- **onMouseOver** applies to HREF links and areas of image maps that can carry links. It is activated when the mouse cursor passes over the object.

Whatever the event handler, the code is attached in the same way – enclose it in "double quotes", assign it with an = sign and put the whole expression inside the tag that creates the object.

If the code contains any text or option settings, it must be enclosed by 'single quotes' instead. So, if you wanted a button click to run the code:

```
alert("Hello there")
```

write it like this:

```
<INPUT TYPE = button VALUE = "Hi" onClick = "alert('Hello there')">
```

## Identifying objects

If you want to change the properties of an object, you must be able to identify it. Some objects are automatically named by the system; others can be named by you as you create them. When referring to an object in your code, you must include its parent object (if any) in the full name, with the property name (if appropriate) at the end; e.g.

```
document.bgColor
```

the background colour of the current document;

```
document.form1.quote.value
```

the *value* property of a textbox named *quote* on the first form on the page.

Here are a couple of event handlers at work. When the button is clicked, it runs the script to change the background colour to black. The (white) 'Told you so!' message then stands out, as does the eyes image, which is drawn in white on a transparent background. Moving the mouse over this image activates the onMouseOver event handler which turn the light on again.

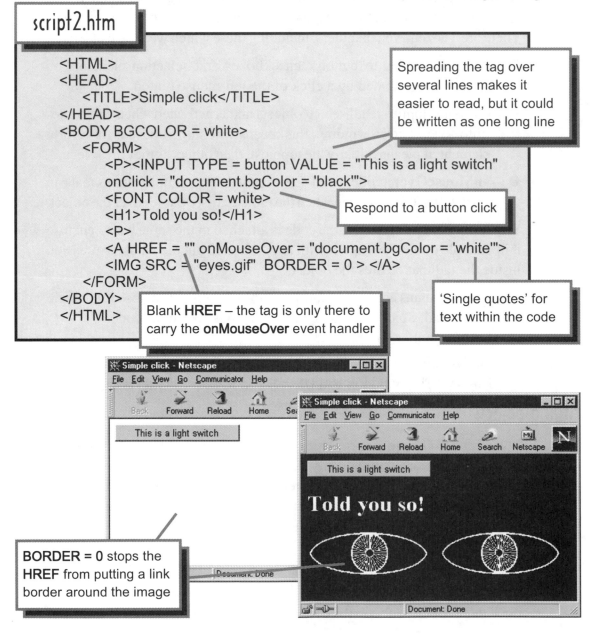

**script2.htm**

```
<HTML>
<HEAD>
    <TITLE>Simple click</TITLE>
</HEAD>
<BODY BGCOLOR = white>
    <FORM>
        <P><INPUT TYPE = button VALUE = "This is a light switch"
        onClick = "document.bgColor = 'black'">
        <FONT COLOR = white>
        <H1>Told you so!</H1>
        <P>
        <A HREF = "" onMouseOver = "document.bgColor = 'white'">
        <IMG SRC = "eyes.gif"  BORDER = 0 > </A>
    </FORM>
</BODY>
</HTML>
```

Spreading the tag over several lines makes it easier to read, but it could be written as one long line

Respond to a button click

'Single quotes' for text within the code

Blank **HREF** – the tag is only there to carry the **onMouseOver** event handler

**BORDER = 0** stops the **HREF** from putting a link border around the image

Simple click - Netscape

This is a light switch

**Told you so!**

156

# The Status line

One common use for JavaScript is to write in the Status line. A static message is easily done – scrolling messages need rather more programming than we have room for here.

The Status line has two properties:

- **defaultStatus = "text"** sets the default message. This is normally used in a BODY script, close to the start of a page.

- **status = "text"** sets a new message in response to an event – perhaps when a text box comes into focus, or the mouse moves over a link.

The Status line is within the Window object, so the name of the target window must be included in the statement. To refer to the current window, you can use either *window* or *self*. These lines are equivalent:

```
onFocus = "self.status = 'Please enter your e-mail address' "
onFocus = "window.status = 'Please enter your e-mail address' "
```

## status and mouse events

If a **status** property is set from an **onMouseOver** or **onMouseOut** event handler, you must include **"return true"** at the end of the code, e.g.

```
onMouseOver="self.status='Go to Yahoo'; return true">
```

There may be a good reason for this or it may just be an accident of JavaScript's design. Don't worry about it, just add in the *return*, separated from the earlier statement by a semi-colon.

In the next example, code in <SCRIPT> </SCRIPT> tags near the top of the **BODY** text sets the default Status line when the page is loaded. Further down you'll find code within an <A HREF = ...> tag that writes a message in the Status line to tell the viewer a little more about that link.

Tip
—
**For a full introduction to JavaScript, try *JavaScript Made Simple*.**

157

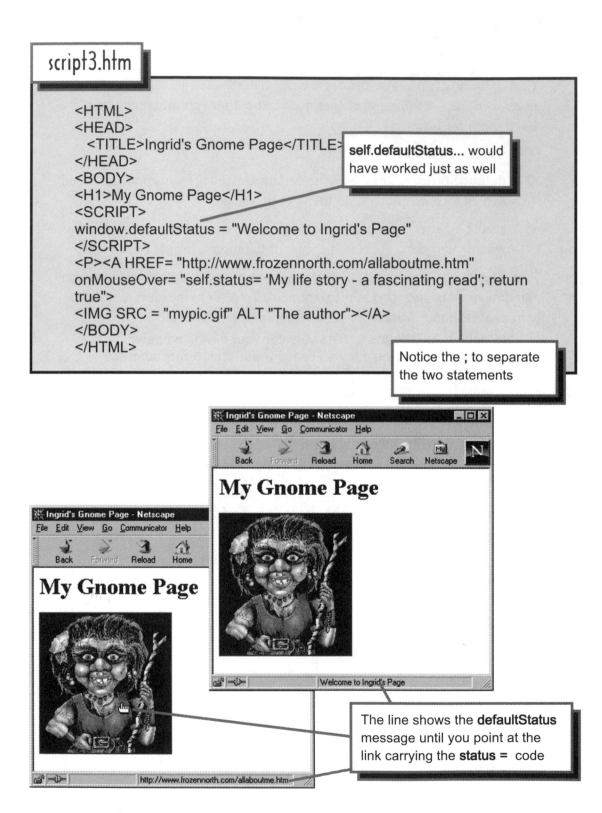

**script3.htm**

```
<HTML>
<HEAD>
  <TITLE>Ingrid's Gnome Page</TITLE>
</HEAD>
<BODY>
<H1>My Gnome Page</H1>
<SCRIPT>
window.defaultStatus = "Welcome to Ingrid's Page"
</SCRIPT>
<P><A HREF= "http://www.frozennorth.com/allaboutme.htm"
onMouseOver= "self.status= 'My life story - a fascinating read'; return
true">
<IMG SRC = "mypic.gif" ALT "The author"></A>
</BODY>
</HTML>
```

**self.defaultStatus...** would have worked just as well

Notice the ; to separate the two statements

*Ingrid's Gnome Page - Netscape*

File  Edit  View  Go  Communicator  Help

Back  Forward  Reload  Home  Search  Netscape

# My Gnome Page

Welcome to Ingrid's Page

*Ingrid's Gnome Page - Netscape*

File  Edit  View  Go  Communicator  Help

Back  Forward  Reload  Home

# My Gnome Page

http://www.frozennorth.com/allaboutme.htm

The line shows the **defaultStatus** message until you point at the link carrying the **status =** code

# Feedback on-line

Writing JavaScript into forms gives you, amongst other things, the ability to respond immediately to your visitors.

When we were looking at custom buttons (page 134) we set one up to calculate the cost of an order. Here's the same form, but this time with the JavaScript to do the calculations. These are handled by a function called *totalCost()*, activated by the onClick event of the *Calculate* button.

```
<BUTTON TYPE=button onClick="totalCost()">
    Calculate cost of order</BUTTON>
```

The function simply multiplies the cost of each item by the number ordered, then adds the costs together. To find out how many have been ordered, it uses the JavaScript function *eval()*, which works out the numerical value of the entry in a text box – giving 0 as the value if the box is empty:

```
surfCost = 9.99 * eval("document.order.surf.value")
```

*surfCost* is a **variable** – a named place in memory in which values can be stored. Unlike some programming languages, you don't have to tell JavaScript to set up variables. It simply recognises that you want to store a value and sets up the space for you.

Once the individual costs have been calculated and stored, the total can be found by adding together the values in the variables.

```
total = surfCost + poseurCost + bikiniCost + vicCost
```

The total cost is now held in the variable total. It can be put onto the screen by setting the value in an **INPUT** text box. One named cost has been added at the bottom of the form for this purpose.

```
<INPUT TYPE = text NAME = cost SIZE = 10>
```

The last line of *totalCost()* copied the total into this box:

```
document.order.cost.value = total
```

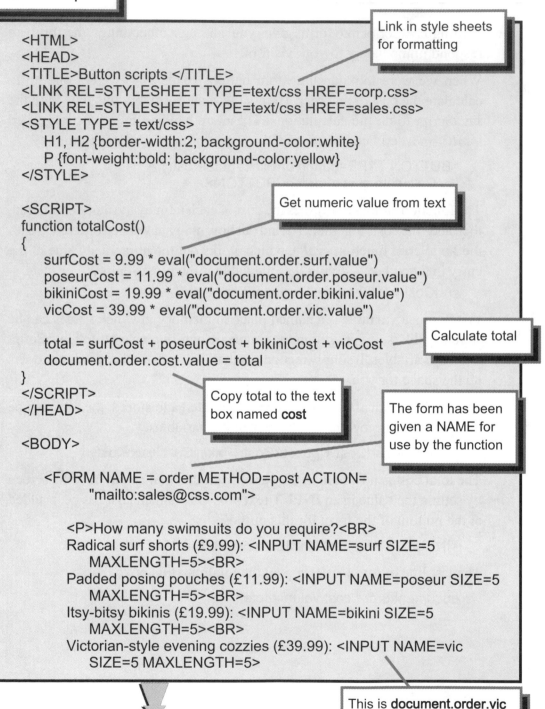

**Button scripts**

Link in style sheets for formatting

```
<HTML>
<HEAD>
<TITLE>Button scripts </TITLE>
<LINK REL=STYLESHEET TYPE=text/css HREF=corp.css>
<LINK REL=STYLESHEET TYPE=text/css HREF=sales.css>
<STYLE TYPE = text/css>
    H1, H2 {border-width:2; background-color:white}
    P {font-weight:bold; background-color:yellow}
</STYLE>

<SCRIPT>
function totalCost()
{
    surfCost = 9.99 * eval("document.order.surf.value")
    poseurCost = 11.99 * eval("document.order.poseur.value")
    bikiniCost = 19.99 * eval("document.order.bikini.value")
    vicCost = 39.99 * eval("document.order.vic.value")

    total = surfCost + poseurCost + bikiniCost + vicCost
    document.order.cost.value = total
}
</SCRIPT>
</HEAD>

<BODY>

    <FORM NAME = order METHOD=post ACTION=
        "mailto:sales@css.com">

    <P>How many swimsuits do you require?<BR>
    Radical surf shorts (£9.99): <INPUT NAME=surf SIZE=5
        MAXLENGTH=5><BR>
    Padded posing pouches (£11.99): <INPUT NAME=poseur SIZE=5
        MAXLENGTH=5><BR>
    Itsy-bitsy bikinis (£19.99): <INPUT NAME=bikini SIZE=5
        MAXLENGTH=5><BR>
    Victorian-style evening cozzies (£39.99): <INPUT NAME=vic
        SIZE=5 MAXLENGTH=5>
```

Get numeric value from text

Calculate total

Copy total to the text box named **cost**

The form has been given a NAME for use by the function

This is **document.order.vic**

**160**

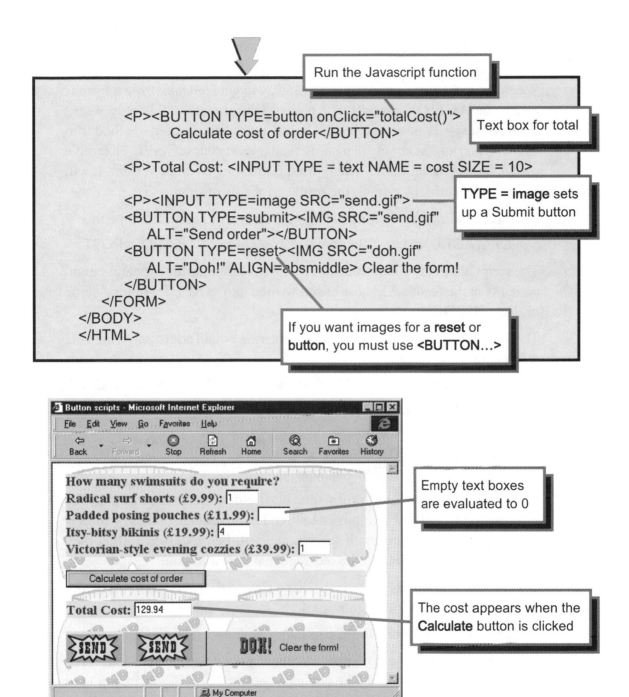

Run the Javascript function

Text box for total

TYPE = image sets up a Submit button

If you want images for a **reset** or **button**, you must use **<BUTTON...>**

```
<P><BUTTON TYPE=button onClick="totalCost()">
    Calculate cost of order</BUTTON>

<P>Total Cost: <INPUT TYPE = text NAME = cost SIZE = 10>

<P><INPUT TYPE=image SRC="send.gif">
<BUTTON TYPE=submit><IMG SRC="send.gif"
    ALT="Send order"></BUTTON>
<BUTTON TYPE=reset><IMG SRC="doh.gif"
    ALT="Doh!" ALIGN=absmiddle> Clear the form!
    </BUTTON>
  </FORM>
</BODY>
</HTML>
```

Empty text boxes are evaluated to 0

The cost appears when the **Calculate** button is clicked

# CGI

## Feedback forms

We noted in Chapter 3 that the simplest way to get feedback from a form is to use the **ACTION = mailto:...** option. Unfortunately, this only works from Netscape. A more reliable, if slightly more complicated, method is to use a CGI script – assuming that one is available on your server. The example shown here is based on the widely-used FormMail, by Matt Wright. It will format and return, by e-mail, the results of the form submission.

To make it work, the opening tag of your form will need a line like this:

```
<FORM ACTION="http://ISP.name/cgi-bin/formmail" METHOD=POST>
```

The script has many options that allow you to customise the appearance and contents of the feedback. These are all written into **<INPUT>** fields – some of them **HIDDEN**.

There must be a **recipient** field. This defines the e-mail address to which the results are to be mailed.

```
<INPUT TYPE=HIDDEN NAME="recipient" VALUE="you@your.ISP">
```

You can include **email** and **realname** fields if you want your visitors to give their names and e-mail addresses.

```
<INPUT type=text NAME="email">
<INPUT type=text NAME="realname">
```

You could collect the same information into fields with other names, and the information would still be returned to you. The advantage of these names is that they are recognised by the script, and will be processed so that they appear in the From: field of the message that it sent to you.

The require field allows you to insist that visitors fill in selected fields before the form is accepted for submission.

```
<INPUT TYPE=hidden NAME="required" value="email,score">
```

In this case, if visitors click **Submit** without giving their e-mail address or the score entry, the form will be bounced back at them. If you are going to use required fields, make it clear on the form that an input is essential!

# Hit counter

A hit counter will record the number of visitors to a page. You can register for a counter with a number of Web sites, but they are increasingly available as CGI scripts through Internet Service Providers. The one illustrated here was created by Muhammad A Muquit.

To pull it into a page, you need code along the lines of:

```
<IMG SRC="http://ISP.name/cgi-bin/Count.cgi?df=username1.dat">
```

The script, Count.cgi, is linked through **<IMG SRC ...>** as it creates an image to show the current number of hits.

A number of options can be written into the code after the '?'. At the very least it needs **df=** followed by the name of the file in which the count is stored. The name is based on your username, and includes a number as you can write counters into several pages if you want to know which are visted most.

Other options allow you to turn on the display of the current date and/or time; add a 3D frame and configure its size and colour; set the number of digits, their display style and characters. The options are written as a continuous stream – no spaces in between – joined by '**&**'. For example:

```
<IMG SRC="http://www.tcp.co.uk/cgi-bin/Count.cgi?md=7&pad=Y
    &ft=12&frgb=255;0;0&df=macbride1.dat" ALIGN=absmiddle>
```

This sets the maximum number of digits to 7 (**md=7**), turns on padding with leading 0s (**pad=Y**), sets the frame thickness to 12 pixels (**ft=12**) and its colour to bright red (**frgb=255;0;0**). When viewed on the Web, it will look like this:

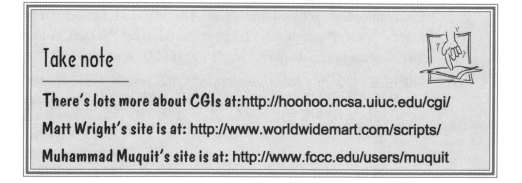

**Take note**

There's lots more about **CGIs** at:http://hoohoo.ncsa.uiuc.edu/cgi/

**Matt Wright's site is at:** http://www.worldwidemart.com/scripts/

**Muhammad Muquit's site is at:** http://www.fccc.edu/users/muquit

# Java applets

If you intend to make a future in programming, Java is a good language to learn, but it is not an easy one. It's not too bad switching to it if you are already an experienced programmer – preferably in C++ – but starting from scratch is hard work. To give you an idea of what's involved in Java programming, here's what it takes to produce a simple scrolling 'banner'. This also shows how Java applets can be configured from within an HTML document – useful background for when we turn to ready-made applets.

A Java program – applet or full-blown application – starts life as a text file, such as the example shown opposite called **MoveText.java**. It scrolls a message across its display area by writing it on the screen then, after a brief delay, overwriting it with a block of colour and rewriting it a little to the left. What you can see is the *source code*. It contains a set of human-readable instructions, using Java keywords, that tell the computer what to do and what order to do it in. This source code must be processed through a compiler, which checks it for errors and – if no errors are found – converts it into machine-readable format and saves it as a file with a **.class** extension. The class file can then be run on any browser, as long as it has Java enabled.

The applet is written into an HTML page with the **<APPLET...>** tag. At its simplest, this gives the filename and the size of the area to display it in, e.g.

```
<APPLET CODE="MoveText.class" WIDTH=500 HEIGHT=200>
</APPLET>
```

## Parameters

Parameters allow you to pass values from HTML into applets – which means that the same applet can be reused to get different effects. MoveText, for example, scrolls text across the screen, and both the message and the speed of movement are set by parameters. This would have been a better – but longer – applet if parameters had been used to set the font, colour, size and other aspects of the display. Here's the HTML that starts it:

```
<APPLET CODE="MoveText.class" WIDTH=500 HEIGHT=200>
    <PARAM NAME = message VALUE = "Special offer - buy now!">
    <PARAM NAME = limit VALUE = 20000>
</APPLET>
```

Delay in milliseconds between movements

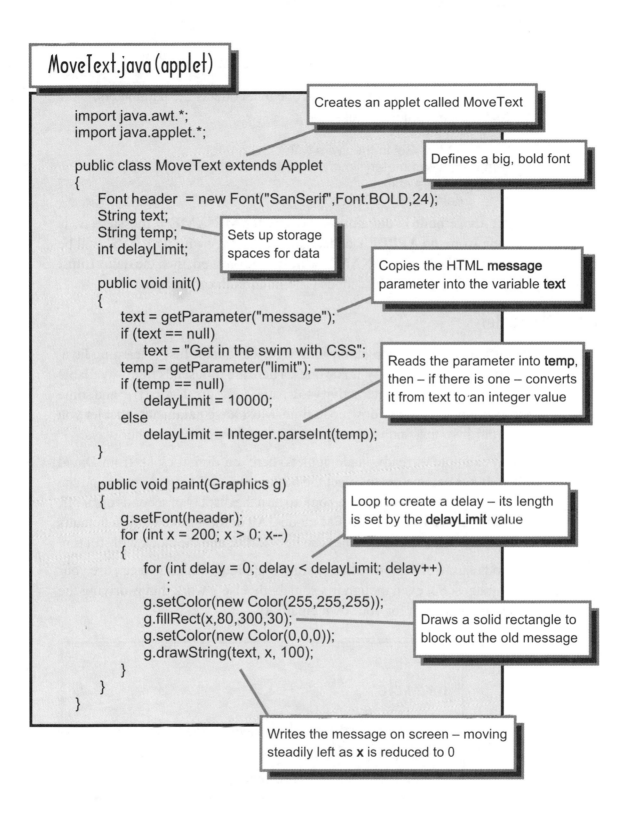

## MoveText.java (applet)

> Creates an applet called MoveText

> Defines a big, bold font

> Sets up storage spaces for data

> Copies the HTML **message** parameter into the variable **text**

> Reads the parameter into **temp**, then – if there is one – converts it from text to an integer value

> Loop to create a delay – its length is set by the **delayLimit** value

> Draws a solid rectangle to block out the old message

> Writes the message on screen – moving steadily left as **x** is reduced to 0

```java
import java.awt.*;
import java.applet.*;

public class MoveText extends Applet
{
    Font header  = new Font("SanSerif",Font.BOLD,24);
    String text;
    String temp;
    int delayLimit;

    public void init()
    {
        text = getParameter("message");
        if (text == null)
            text = "Get in the swim with CSS";
        temp = getParameter("limit");
        if (temp == null)
            delayLimit = 10000;
        else
            delayLimit = Integer.parseInt(temp);
    }

    public void paint(Graphics g)
    {
        g.setFont(header);
        for (int x = 200; x > 0; x--)
        {
            for (int delay = 0; delay < delayLimit; delay++)
                ;
            g.setColor(new Color(255,255,255));
            g.fillRect(x,80,300,30);
            g.setColor(new Color(0,0,0));
            g.drawString(text, x, 100);
        }
    }
}
```

And here's crucial part of the Java code that collects the parameters:

```
text = getParameter("message");
    if (text == null)
        text = "Get in the swim with CSS";
temp = getParameter("limit");
    if (temp == null)
        delayLimit = 10000;
```

Notice those built-in defaults. If the **<PARAM NAME = message ...** is missing from the **APPLET** code, then 'Get in the swim with CSS' will be displayed. If **<PARAM NAME = limit ...** is omitted, then the **delayLimit** will be set to 10000 milliseconds (one-hundredth of a second).

## Ready-made applets

If you want the fizz of applets on your page, without the fuss of learning Java, the solution is to use ready-made ones. There are thousands freely available on the Web. Some add interactivity to a page; some are decorative; and some are a complete waste of download time. Most have parameters that let you add your own text and images, or customise the display in other ways.

As an example of ready-made applets, here's a digital clock from David Zhao. It has parameters to select the background colour and image and the digits images, to adjust the time zone, to turn the display of seconds on or off, and to run it in 24 hour or AM/PM modes. All of these have built-in defaults – any or all of the **PARAM** lines can be omitted, and the clock will still run.

A good feature of this – as of other similar applets – is that you can use your own images. So, even though it's somebody else's work that is driving the show, there's room for your own creativity.

## Take note

If you want to write your own applets, you'll need the Java Development Kit from Javasoft at http://www.javasoft.com – and a copy of *Java Made Simple* from any good bookshop!

## Digital clock in Java

```
<HTML>
<HEAD>
<TITLE>Java Clock</TITLE>
<!-- Java code by David Zhao, images by Mac -->
</HEAD>
<BODY>
<APPLET CODE=dclock.class WIDTH=200 HEIGHT=60>
    <PARAM NAME=bgcolor VALUE= "000000">
    <PARAM NAME=digits VALUE="roman.gif">
    <PARAM NAME=background VALUE="slab.gif">
    <PARAM NAME=timezone VALUE="00">
    <PARAM NAME=seconds VALUE="no">
    <PARAM NAME=24hour VALUE="no">
    </APPLET>
</BODY>
</HTML>
```

Digits image

Background image

Both default to **yes**

The resulting display – a digital clock with roman numerals!!

The digits image – the code slices numerals from the strip

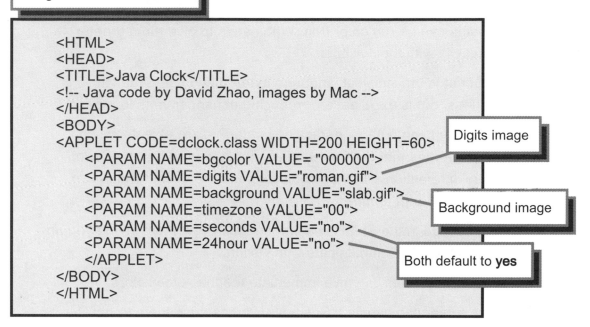

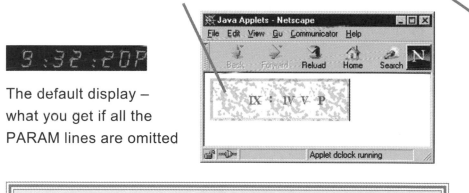

The default display – what you get if all the PARAM lines are omitted

.
I
II
III
IV
V
VI
VII
VIII
IX

:
A
P

## Take note

You can find this applet – and around 300 others – at the Java Boutique (http://www.javasoft.com) or get it directly from its author's site (http://www.siusa.com/dclock/)

**167**

# Summary

❑ Programs can be run on or from Web pages to give them greater interactivity with their visitors.

❑ JavaScript is the simplest language to learn and use. It has its limitations, but is excellent for producing enhancements to a page.

❑ The elements on a page, particularly in forms, are objects which have properties that can be recognised and altered by JavaScript. Visitors' interaction with these objects generate events which can trigger JavaScript routines.

❑ The message in the Status line can be easily rewritten, giving you an additional way to communicate with visitors.

❑ JavaScript routines can give immediate feedback to visitors.

❑ If your server can handle CGI scripts, you can use them to get feedback from forms, run hit counters, and more.

❑ Java is a fully-fledged programming language. If you don't have the time or energy to master it, there are many ready-made applets available on the Internet, and you can adapt these to add interactivity to your pages.

# 10 Publishing your pages

Organising your files ............ 170

Keywords .................... 172

Uploading with WS_FTP ......... 174

Publishing wizards ............. 176

Summary .................... 178

# Organising your files

## Links within the site

OK, so you've created all your pages, but do they work together as a site? Will a visitor be able to tell what's available and reach any given page easily? Is there an index, table of contents or other means of navigating the site? Are related pages linked from one point? Is every page linked in somewhere? Can your visitors get back to the main index quickly?

There are no hard and fast rules about how to structure a site, but you should have your pages linked along these kind of lines.

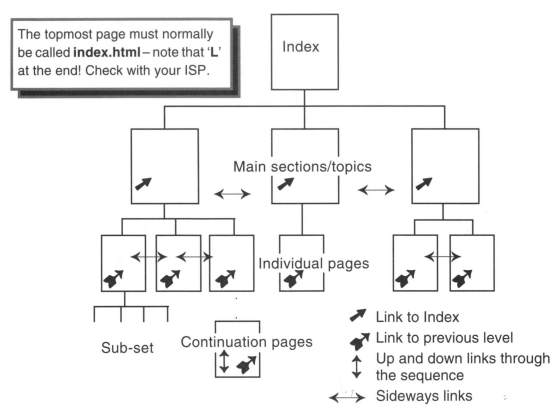

The topmost page must normally be called **index.html** – note that '**L**' at the end! Check with your ISP.

Index

Main sections/topics

Individual pages

Sub-set    Continuation pages

↗ Link to Index
↗ Link to previous level
↕ Up and down links through the sequence
↔ Sideways links

You must have a top-level index page, but how much of the rest of this structure is used will depend upon the information that you want to convey. A sequence of pages is only really useful for a story or other truly continuous text – and even here there should be an index so that visitors can jump into the sequence at any point.

## Folders and paths

If you have a relatively small, simple set of pages – perhaps no more than a couple of dozen files in total – then you can store them conveniently in a single folder. Much larger than this, and it will be easier to manage them if they are in a set of folders. You might have one folder for each topic or section, or you might organise by type, storing pages in one folder, images in a second and other files in a third – or a combination of both.

If you are using several folders, your files must be stored in the same structure of folders on the server, or your path/filename links won't work. This shouldn't be too much of a problem as you can upload complete folders with the publishing wizards or WS_FTP (see the next few pages) – but if you are uploading any other way, do check that folders are being created properly, and make them yourself if necessary.

## Throw out the rubbish!

Clean up the folders before you upload. There are bound to be some test pages, drafts, unwanted images and other files that were used at an early stage but then rejected from the final system. You do not want to upload these – they are a waste of Web space. If you are not sure if some files are unwanted, transfer them to a temporary folder and browse right through your site, checking all the linked pages, images and other files.

## Talk to your ISP

Before you go much further, talk to your Internet Service Provider. Find out the URL of your Web space and what name you should give to your home (topmost) page – it will normally be 'index.html'.

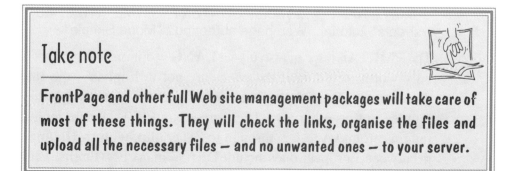

### Take note

FrontPage and other full Web site management packages will take care of most of these things. They will check the links, organise the files and upload all the necessary files – and no unwanted ones – to your server.

# Keywords

The **<META>** tag allows you to write labelled information into your documents. Its main use is in supplying keywords for search engines and Internet directories. Most search engines have 'crawlers' which patrol the Web constantly, looking for new material. When one finds your home page it will record the title and use any keywords that are present to index it. Similarly, some directories look for classification data when you register your URL with them. If you want people to find your site as they browse the Web, make sure that you include good **META** information.

The basic tag takes the form:

```
<META NAME = ... CONTENT = ...>
```

The NAME identifies the type of information. It can be anything, but the following are widely recognised:

> **keywords** for indexing by search engines;
>
> **classification** for cataloguing by directories;
>
> **description** shown after the title when the page is found and listed by some engines and directories;
>
> **author** often also shown in the **<ADDRESS>** in the body of the page;
>
> **date** of last modification to the site – important, as some search engines allow people to search by date.

The **CONTENT** is any appropriate text. For keywords and classification data, it should be a comma separated list of words or "phrases in double quotes" which identify the subject matter of the site.

For example, the top page of the online version of this book has this tag:

```
<META NAME = keywords CONTENT = HTML, "HTML 4.0", "style
sheets", tutorial, "Web page authoring", "Made Simple">
```

The **<META>** tag can also take a **LANG =** option, though this is probably only worth including if the pages are not in English – the Internet is so dominated by English that it is normally assumed that pages are written in it unless it says otherwise. There are around 150 standard language codes, ranging from AA (Afar) through to ZU (Zulu), with IK (Inupiak, Eskimo) in between. European ones include DE (German), EN (English), ES (Spanish)

FR (French), IT (Italian) and NL (Dutch). You can read the full list at:

http://www.oasis-open.org/cover/iso639a.html

If you were running a bilingual site advertising holiday homes in France, you would want **META** tags along these lines:

```
<META NAME = keywords LANG = en
  CONTENT = France, "holiday homes", holiday, vacation>
<META NAME = description LANG = en CONTENT = "A fine
  selection of holiday homes throughout France."
<META NAME=keywords LANG=fr
  CONTENT=France, gites,vacances>
<META NAME = description LANG = fr CONTENT = "Gites et
maisons pour les vacances en tous r&eacute;gions de France."
```

That's **régions** in the last line. If you need to include accented letters anywhere in an HTML document, you must use the special character entities (see page 188).

# Registering your site

The simple fact of having keywords on your home page will ensure that your page is indexed by some search engines – including AltaVista, HotBot and Infoseek – though it may take a little while before you are included. If you want to be listed in the directories, you normally have to go to them and register your URL. Here's what you must do at the big three.

### Yahoo

Work your way through the directory until you reach the section where your site fits best, then follow the link <u>Suggest a site</u> at the bottom of the page. You will have to supply your URL and contact information, a description of the site and any alternative categories. At some point, someone from Yahoo will visit the site and may, or may not, decide to include it.

### Lycos

Click on <u>Add a Site</u> on the main page and give your URL and e-mail address.

### Excite

Click on <u>Submit URL</u> on the main page and give your URL and e-mail address, plus the title, description and keywords for your site.

# Uploading with WS_FTP

FTP (File Transfer Protocol) is the standard method of transferring files across the Internet. Browsers can download files using FTP, but not upload. For uploading – and more efficient downloading, you need WS_FTP. If you haven't got a copy, you can get one from the home site of its author at:

> http://www.ipswitch.com

If you have used FTP before, it will probably have been to connect to one of the FTP archives. Here, you log in as 'Anonymous', giving your e-mail name as a password. At these sites you can download from directories (the same as *folders* in Windows) and upload to designated incoming ones, but you cannot create new directories or rename or delete files. When you login to your own directory on your provider's system you have far more control.

## Accessing your Web space

1   Login to your service, then run WS_FTP. It should start with the **Session Properties** panel open – if it isn't, click **Connect** to open it.

2   Click **New**, then type in a **Profile name** for the connection – this can be anything that is meaningful to you.

3   For the **Host name**, enter the name of your provider's FTP server. The **User ID** is the same as the first part of your e-mail name. The **Password** is your standard login password.

4   You can change directory after you have logged in, but it is simpler to do it now. If you have been given the path to your directory at the ISP, switch to the **Startup** panel and enter it into the **Initial Remote Host Directory** slot.

5   Enter the path to the home page files in the **Initial Local Directory** slot.

6   Click **OK** to move to the main screen. You are ready to upload.

174

# Uploading

As WS_FTP establishes the connection, you should see messages scrolling through the bottom panel. You will know that you are connected and ready to upload when the messages stop. You may see your directory's name (or '/' which shows you are at the top level directory) in the *Remote System* slot at the top, and if you have already uploaded some files they will be listed.

Select **Auto** – pages are then automatically transferred as Text and other files as Binary. Select the files, and sub-folders (if any) in your home page directory, and click →  to send them to the remote system.

With larger files, you will see a **Transfer Status** panel, displaying the progress of the uploading. HTML files are normally so small and transfer so quickly that all you see is a flash on the screen.

Transfer Status
Sending BINARY file tyint.gif (26195 bytes)
13%
3584 : 27.41 Kbps : 0:01 : 0:08        Cancel

The whole set shouldn't take more than a few minutes to upload. After the last one has gone in, the directory listing on the Remote System pane will update. Check that they are all there, and if they are, click **Close** to shut down the FTP connection and click **Exit** to close WS_FTP.

Here I'm just uploading a few files to update the site

175

# Publishing wizards

## Publishing from Netscape Composer

The publishing facility in Composer is easy to use, but limited. In any one uploading session, all the selected files are transferred to the same directory, wherever they were stored on your local system. So, if you have set up a structure of subfolders locally, you must first use WS_FTP to create the same structure on the remote system, before copying over files, one folder at a time. In practice, publishing from Composer only makes sense if all your files are in one folder, or if you are uploading the odd file to update your site.

Start Composer and open the page you want to publish. Use the **File – Publish** command, or click the **Publish** icon to open the dialog box.

The essential information – filename, FTP location, your user name and password – go into the top half of the dialog box. Much of this information is stored, so that next time you will only need to enter the page and filename (if different).

If there are **Other files to include**, start by selecting **Files associated with this page** – to get the images and other embedded files – or **All files in page's folder**. You can then click **Select All** or [Ctrl]- or [Shift]-click on the displayed list if you only want new or changed files.

Uploading a page and its associated files all at once is convenient, but they must all be in the same folder for the links to work once they are up (in the same folder) in your Web space.

176

# Microsoft Web publishing wizard

FrontPage Express has a Web publishing wizard – and for non-FrontPage Express users, the same wizard can be downloaded from Microsoft's free-stuff area. It is as easy to use as Netscape's publishing routine, and while it doesn't have that neat **Files associated with this page** option, it does let you upload subfolders – creating them as necessary in your Web space.

The wizard has special routines for CompuServe, AOL, and other major providers. Users of other services have to do a little more work – the main job being to contact your ISP and find the URL of your Web space. This can be the **ftp://** address of your space on their server, or the **http://** address of your home page – the wizard normally works just as well with either URL.

When you run the wizard, supply the information requested on each panel, clicking **Next** after each, until you reach this panel.

If you are uploading for the first time, simply select the folder and tick **Include subfolders**.

If you are updating the site with a few new files, click **Browse Files** and select the ones that you want to upload.

# Summary

❑ The files that you need for your Web site should be carefully organised so that you know where everything is.

❑ Check that all the links work properly – taking extra care if your files are arranged in a set of subfolders.

❑ Remove unused files from your Web page folders – it's just a waste of space to upload them.

❑ Before finalising your site, talk to your ISP to find out what the home page should be called and how to access your Web space.

❑ Credits and keywords can be added to a page through the <META> tag. The keywords will help to ensure that your site is picked up by Internet search engines.

❑ To have your site listed at some Internet directories, you must visit them and register your site.

❑ The most efficient way to upload your Web files and to organise your Web space is with WS_FTP.

❑ The publishing wizard in Composer and the Microsoft Web publishing wizard both offer a simple, but limited, way to upload files.

# Reference section

Tags and options . . . . . . . . . . . . . . .180

Character codes . . . . . . . . . . . . . . .188

Style sheets . . . . . . . . . . . . . . . .189

Links . . . . . . . . . . . . . . . . . . . .193

# Tags and options

All tags should have closing tags except where indicated: S = single tag
O = closing tag optional. **(4.0)** indicates the tag is new in HTML 4.0.

## Structure

**\<HTML\>** (p.6) defines the document as HTML.

**\<HEAD\>** (p.6) marks the HEAD area. Its text is not displayed on screen.

**\<TITLE\>** (p.6) text to appear in the browser's Title bar, and as the page title in search engines. Goes in the HEAD area.

S    **\<META NAME = ... LANG = ... CONTENT = ...\>** (p.172) used to provide labelled information. These NAME values are generally recognised:

> **Author** – name of page's author;
>
> **Keywords** – comma separated list of words or "phrases in quotes" for use by search engines;
>
> **Categories** – list of words or "phrases" for use by Web directories.

**LANG** specifies the language using standard abreviations, e.g. en = English, fr = French, sp = Spanish.

S    **\<BASE HREF = ...\>** (p.43) URL to which all HREFs are appended, e.g. with the BASE set at *www.mysite.com/products* the HREF *specials.htm* would be interpreted as *www.mysite.com/product/specials.htm*.

If omitted, the page's URL (minus its filename) is taken as the BASE.

**\<BODY BACKGROUND = ... BGCOLOR = ... TEXT = ... LINK = ... VLINK = ... ALINK = ...\>** (p.6, 30) defines the BODY area. Optional settings for the background image or colours for the background, body text, unvisited, visited and active links.

S    **\<FRAMESET ROWS = ...** *or* **COLS = ...** **\>** (p.92) defines the structure of a framed system, dividing an area into columns or rows.

The size of the columns or rows may be set in pixels, a percentage of the window or '*' indicating equal shares of remaining space.

**\<NOFRAMES\>** marks the code to be displayed if the browser cannot handle frames.

**<FRAME NAME = ... SRC = ... FRAMEBORDER = 1/0** (on or off)
**BORDERCOLOR = ... MARGINWIDTH = ... MARGINHEIGHT =
... NORESIZE SCROLLING = auto/yes/no>** (p.92) defines a frame.

NAME is a TARGET for HREFs; SRC is the initial page to be displayed;
margin sizes can be set in pixels or a percentage of the frame; NORESIZE
fixes the window size; SCROLLING controls the presence of scroll bars.

**<IFRAME ...>** Opens a frame within a paragraph or other element in a page.
Options as <FRAME>.

# Text formatting

All formatting tags can take the **ID = ... CLASS = ...** or **STYLE = ...** options
to apply style sheet formats to the element.

**<DIV LANG= ... TITLE = ... ALIGN = ...>** (p.115) marks a block for
formatting.

**<SPAN>** (p.115) marks code within a paragraph or other element for
formatting. Options as <DIV>.

◄O    **<P>** (p.20) paragraph, with a clear line above and below. Options as <DIV>.

S►    **<BR>** (p.20) starts a new line of text, without leaving a blank line above.

**<H1>** to **<H6>** (p.21) headings, with 1 the largest. Options as <DIV>.

**<ADDRESS>** (p.26) small italic format normally used for contact
information.

**<FONT SIZE = ... COLOR = ... FACE = ... >** (p.28, 30, 32) defines the
font for all subsequent text. SIZE can be a number between 1 and 7, or a
relative value (e.g. −1, +2); COLOR is a colour name or hexadecimal value;
FACE is followed by a comma separated list of font names.

S►    **<BASEFONT SIZE = ... COLOR = ... FACE = ...>** (p.28) sets the default
font.

**<CENTER>** (p.23) centres enclosed text and images.

**<B>** bold.

**<I>** italic.

**<U>** underline

**<BIG>** set to 'large' font size as defined by the browser.

**<S>** *or* **<STRIKE>** strikethrough.

**<SMALL>** set to 'small' font size as defined by the browser.

**<TT>** use TypewriTer (`Courier`) font.

**<SUB>** subscript.

**<SUP>** superscript.

**<PRE>** (p.27) displays pre-formatted text, with spaces, tabs and line breaks as written in the HTML code.

**<BLOCKQUOTE>** (p.26) displays text indented from both margins.

(4.0)   **<Q>** as <BLOCKQUOTE>.

S➤   **<HR ALIGN = ... SIZE = ... WIDTH = ... NOSHADE>** (p.21) draws a horizontal rule, with a 3-D effect unless NOSHADE is given. SIZE is its depth in pixels, WIDTH is set in pixels or percentage of the window.

# Phrasal elements

These format the appearance, but are mainly intended for marking up text for analysis by other programs.

(4.0)   **<ACRONYM TITLE = ...>** displayed as ordinary text. TITLE is what the acronym stands for.

**<CITE>** used for quotations, displayed in italics.

**<CODE>** used for samples of program code, displayed in Courier.

**<DFN>** used for definitions, displayed as normal text.

**<EM>** used for emphasis, usually displayed in italics.

**<KBD>** used to indicate keyboard input by user, displayed in Courier.

**<SAMP>** used for sample outputs from programs, displayed in Courier.

**<STRONG>** used for stronger emphasis, displayed in bold.

**<VAR>** used for program variables, displayed in italics.

**182**

# Lists

**<OL TYPE = ... COMPACT START = ...>** (p.34) ordered (numbered) list. The TYPE sets the numbering style: 1 = numbers; a = lower case letters; A = capital letters; i = lower case roman numerals; I = capital roman numerals. A START number can be given. If set, the COMPACT option reduces the spacing between items.

**<UL TYPE =** *disc/circle/square* **COMPACT>** (p.34) unordered (bulleted) list. The TYPE sets the bullet style.

O  **<LI TYPE = VALUE = ...>** (p.34) item in a list. The TYPE can be set to vary the bullet or numbering style. A VALUE can be given in an ordered list to restart the numbering sequence.

**<DL COMPACT>** (p.34) definition list.

O  **<DT>** (p.34) item to be defined.

O  **<DD>** (p.34) definition, displayed indented beneath its item.

# Links

**<A HREF =** *url* **or A NAME = ...>** (p.38, 40) anchors for hyperlinks. HREF identifies a page or NAMEd place to jump to, or other Internet resource, defined by *url*; NAME labels a point within a page.

S  **<LINK REL= ... or REV = ... TYPE = ... HREF= ... MEDIA = ... TARGET = ...>** (p.120) sets up a variety of links. The key one is REL = STYLESHEET, used to link in an external style sheet.

**<BASE TARGET=...>** (p.95) sets the URL to be prefixed to links on the page.

# Images and image maps

S  **<IMG  SRC =** *url* **ALT = ... ALIGN = ... HEIGHT = ... WIDTH = ... BORDER = ... HSPACE = ... VSPACE = ... USEMAP = ... ISMAP = ...>** (p.60) incorporates an image, identified by *url*. HEIGHT and WIDTH can be set in pixels or a percentage of the window size; BORDER is set in pixels and will be in the current font colour; HSPACE and VSPACE create space around the image (size in pixels); USEMAP names the image for use with MAP, when the image map is to be run from the browser; ISMAP is used for server-side image maps.

**<MAP NAME = ...>** (p.66) links to the image named by **<IMG ... USEMAP ...>**

S➤    **<AREA HREF=** *url* **TARGET = ... ALT = ... SHAPE =** *rect/circ/poly* **COORDS = ...>** (p.66) defines a hyperlink in an image map. If the SHAPE is a *rect*(angle), the COORDS are of the top left and bottom right corners; for a *circ*(le), give the centre point and radius; for a *poly*(gon), the coordinates of all the vertices, repeating the first at the end to close the outline. If a TARGET is not given, the linked page will be displayed in the current window.

# Forms

**<FORM ACTION = ... METHOD = POST>** (p.124) marks a form. The ACTION can be mailto:... for simple e-mail feedback (from Navigator only) or the URL of a server-side script – normally a CGI.

All form elements can take the options **DISABLED** (turning it off) and **TABINDEX = ...** (setting the order in which [Tab] presses move through the elements).

S➤    **<INPUT TYPE = ... NAME = ... VALUE = ... CHECKED = ... READONLY = ... SIZE = ... MAXLENGTH = ... SRC = ... ALT = ... USEMAP = ... ID = ... >** (p.127) creates different input elements, with varying options, depending upon the TYPE setting:

*text* single line text box; can take options SIZE (display width in characters) and MAXLENGTH (input limit in characters)

*password* as text, but input displayed as asterisks

*checkbox* on/off selector. If checked, the NAME/VALUE pair is submitted with the form.

*radio* used to select between alternatives, all of which have the same NAME but different VALUEs. Only the selected NAME/VALUE pair is submitted.

*submit* creates a 'submit' button. Its caption can be set by VALUE.

*reset* creates a button to clear or reset the fields. Use the VALUE option to change its caption.

*file* allows a file to be submitted with the form.

*hidden* does not appear in the display. Used for control fields.

*image* creates a clickable image. The coordinates of the clicked point are submitted with the form, and could be processed by a program at the server. The <BUTTON> tag is a better way to add images.

*button* creates a 'blank' button. Its caption is set by VALUE and its effect determined by JavaScript code running from *onclick*.

**(4.0)** **<LABEL for = field_id>** (p.136) links a text label to the <INPUT> element with the given ID, so that selecting the label also selects the control. Improves accessibility when the form is rendered non-visually.

**(4.0)** **<BUTTON NAME = ... VALUE = ... TYPE = *button/submit/reset*>** (p.133) alternative to <INPUT TYPE = image ...> for incorporating clickable images in forms.

**<TEXTAREA NAME = ... ROWS = ... COLS = ...>** (p.127) creates a multi-line text box.

**<SELECT NAME = ... SIZE – ... MULTIPLE>** (p.131) sets up a clickable list of options, each defined by an <OPTION> tag. SIZE is the number of visible rows; MULTIPLE allows multiple selections.

O  **<OPTION VALUE = ... SELECTED>** (p.131) defines an option in a SELECT list. The tag must be followed by the text to be displayed in the list.

**(4.0)** **<FIELDSET>** (p.135) groups a set of fields, which can be named by a LEGEND tag. Can improve accessibility by enabling a non-visual browser to describe the form better.

**(4.0)** **<LEGEND ALIGN = *top/bottom/left/right*>** (p.135) sets the position of the LEGEND text in a FIELDSET.

## Tables

**<TABLE   ALIGN = ... BGCOLOR = ... WIDTH = ... COLS = ... BORDER = ... FRAME = ... RULES = ... CELLSPACING = ... CELLPADDING = ...>** (p.74) defines a table. ALIGN and WIDTH are relative to the window; COLS tells the browser how many columns there are;

BORDER, CELLSPACING and CELL PADDING are set in pixels; FRAME and RULES determine which frame and inner lines are drawn.

**\<CAPTION ALIGN = *top/bottom/left/right*\>** (p.74) sets a caption above the table, or elsewhere if the ALIGN option is used.

O   **\<TR BGCOLOR = ...\>** (p.74) defines a row in a table.

O   **\<TD BGCOLOR = ... ROWSPAN = ... COLSPAN = ... NOWRAP\>** (p.74) defines a table data cell. Can be set to span more than one row or column if required. NOWRAP cancels text wrapping to the next line.

O   **\<TH\>** defines a table header cell. Options as for \<TD\>.

**(4.0)**  O **\<COLGROUP SPAN = ... WIDTH = ...\>** (p.84) defines a groups of columns in a table. SPAN is the number of columns; WIDTH the size, in pixels, of each.

**(4.0)** S   **\<COL SPAN = ... WIDTH = ...\>** (p.84) marks each column in a group. SPAN here sets how many columns are spanned by the current one – and SPAN=0 means *all* remaining columns in the group; WIDTH sets the size in pixels.

O   **\<THEAD\>** (p.82) header information in a table, enables more efficient printing and database analysis.

O   **\<TFOOT\>** (p.82) follows \<THEAD\>, and provides footer information.

O   **\<TBODY\>** (p.82) follows \<TFOOT\>, contains the code for the main table.

# Active sheets

**\<STYLE TYPE = ... MEDIA = ... TITLE = ...\>** (p.101) marks the code containing style definitions. The TYPE is normally text/css. MEDIA is assumed to be the screen but can be any number of the following, given as a comma separated list: *screen, print, projection, braille, speech* (synthesizer) or *all*.

**\<APPLET CODEBASE = *url* CODE = *class_file* ALT = ... NAME = ... WIDTH = ... HEIGHT = ... ALIGN = ...\>** (p.164) embeds a Java applet into a page. The applet's working area is defined by its WIDTH and HEIGHT, given in pixels or percentage of the window. ALT provides a description for browsers that are not Java-enabled; NAME is only needed if there are several applets in the page and they communicate with each other.

S➤ **\<PARAM NAME = ... VALUE = ...>** (p.166) given within an \<APPLET> pair to pass parameter data to an applet.

**\<SCRIPT TYPE = ... SRC = *url*>** (p.153) embeds a script in a page. Strictly, the TYPE should be given in the form "text/javascript", "text/vbscript", but JavaScript is assumed otherwise. SRC = allows you to link to an external file instead of using code within the document.

**\<NOSCRIPT>** contains text to be displayed on those browsers which cannot run the associated script.

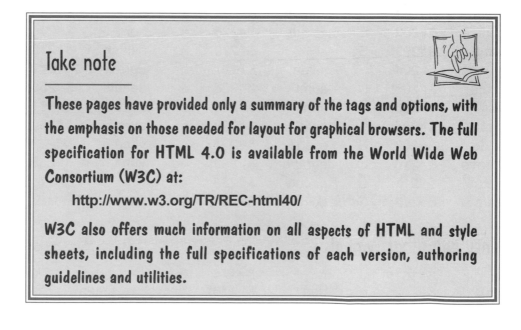

## Take note

These pages have provided only a summary of the tags and options, with the emphasis on those needed for layout for graphical browsers. The full specification for HTML 4.0 is available from the World Wide Web Consortium (W3C) at:

http://www.w3.org/TR/REC-html40/

W3C also offers much information on all aspects of HTML and style sheets, including the full specifications of each version, authoring guidelines and utilities.

# Character codes

HTML pages travel across the Web as pure text files, which means that characters outside the standard ASCII set are not recognised. To include accented letters and other symbols, use these character codes, or *entities*, giving either the name or the number. In either case, the code must have ampersand before and semicolon after, e.g. **&Agrave;**.

## Accented letters

| | | | | | | | | |
|---|---|---|---|---|---|---|---|---|
| Agrave | &#192; | À | Otilde | &#213; | Õ | euml | &#235; | ë |
| Aacute | &#193; | Á | Ouml | &#214; | Ö | igrave | &#236; | ì |
| Acirc | &#194; | Â | Oslash | &#216; | Ø | iacute | &#237; | í |
| Atilde | &#195; | Ã | Ugrave | &#217; | Ù | icirc | &#238; | î |
| Auml | &#196; | Ä | Uacute | &#218; | Ú | iuml | &#239; | ï |
| Aring | &#197; | Å | Ucirc | &#219; | Û | ntilde | &#241; | ñ |
| AElig | &#198; | Æ | Uuml | &#220; | Ü | ograve | &#242; | ò |
| Ccedil | &#199; | Ç | Yacute | &#221; | Ý | oacute | &#243; | ó |
| Egrave | &#200; | È | szlig | &#223; | ß | ocirc | &#244; | ô |
| Eacute | &#201; | É | agrave | &#224; | à | otilde | &#245; | õ |
| Ecirc | &#202; | Ê | aacute | &#225; | á | ouml | &#246; | ö |
| Euml | &#203; | Ë | acirc | &#226; | â | oslash | &#248; | ø |
| Igrave | &#204; | Ì | atilde | &#227; | ã | ugrave | &#249; | ù |
| Iacute | &#205; | Í | auml | &#228; | ä | uacute | &#250; | ú |
| Icirc | &#206; | Î | aring | &#229; | å | ucirc | &#251; | û |
| Iuml | &#207; | Ï | aelig | &#230; | æ | uuml | &#252; | ü |
| Ntilde | &#209; | Ñ | ccedil | &#231; | ç | yacute | &#253; | ý |
| Ograve | &#210; | Ò | egrave | &#232; | è | yuml | &#255; | ÿ |
| Oacute | &#211; | Ó | eacute | &#233; | é | | | |
| Ocirc | &#212; | Ô | ecirc | &#234; | ê | | | |

## Currency and other symbols

| | | | | | | | | |
|---|---|---|---|---|---|---|---|---|
| iexcl | &#161; | ¡ | reg | &#174; | ® | iquest | &#191; | ¿ |
| cent | &#162; | ¢ | deg | &#176; | ° | times | &#215; | × |
| pound | &#163; | £ | plusmn | &#177; | ± | divide | &#247; | ÷ |
| curren | &#164; | ¤ | micro | &#181; | µ | quot | &#34; | " |
| yen | &#165; | ¥ | frac14 | &#188; | ¼ | amp | &#38; | & |
| brvbar | &#166; | ¦ | frac12 | &#189; | ½ | lt | &#60; | < |
| copy | &#169; | © | frac34 | &#190; | ¾ | gt | &#62; | > |

# Style sheets

## HTML tags and options

**\<STYLE TYPE = text/css\> ... \</STYLE\>** to enclose a style definition block in an HTML document.

**\<LINK REL=STYLESHEET TYPE=text/css HREF = url\>** to create link to a style sheet, marked with a .css extension.

**@import urlurl or filename);** alternative way to link to a style sheet.

**...TYPE = text/css STYLE = *"style definitions"*** ... can be used within most tags to define a style within the BODY of a document.

**CLASS = *classname*** used within a tag to select a class definition for that tag.

**ID = *idname*** also used within a tag to select a named definition for that tag.

**\<DIV ...\> ... \</DIV\>** encloses a set of elements within a page for styling. Styles can be defined directly within the \<DIV\> tag, or indirectly through a CLASS or ID option.

**\<SPAN\> ... \</SPAN\>** as \<DIV\>, but enclosing an area within an element.

## Attributes and settings

In this summary:

- keywords used for settings are shown in *italics*;
- sizes can be given in units of em (size of letter 'm'), cm or px (pixels), unless otherwise stated;
- colours can be given as names or by *rgb(red_val, green_val, blue_val)* where values are numbers in the range 0 to 255
- the *none* setting is used to turn off settings that may have been inherited from a parent element or earlier definition of an element.

Take note

Only newer browsers can handle style sheets.

189

# Font

**font-family**: font names (in "quotes" if they contain spaces) with a generic name as last alternative. The generic names are *serif, sans-serif, cursive, fantasy, monospace.*

**font-style**: *normal, italic* or *oblique.*

**font-variant**: *normal* or *small-caps.*

**font-weight**: *normal, bold, bolder, lighter,* or a value 100, 200 … to 900.

**font-size**: *xx-small, x-small, small, medium, large, x-large, xx-large, larger, smaller,* a percentage value or size in points (*pt*).

**font**: list of values for all or some of font-style, font-variant, font-weight, font-size and font-family.

**color**: colour_value.

# Background

**background-color**: colour_value or *transparent.*

**background-image**: *url*(hyperlink or filename) or *none.*

**background-repeat**: *repeat, repeat-x, repeat-y* or *no-repeat.*

**background-attachment**: *scroll* or *fixed.*

**background-position**: distance_from_top, distance_from_left as percentage or size; or keywords *top, center* or *bottom, left, center* or *right.*

**background**: list of values for background-color; background-image; background-repeat; background-attachment; background-position.

# Text properties

**word-spacing**: *normal* or value in ems

**letter-spacing**: *normal* or value in ems

**text-align**: *left, right, center* or *justify.*

**vertical-align**: *baseline, sub, super, text-top, middle, text-bottom,* sets alignment relative to the parent element – could be used to pick out a word in a paragraph.

**text-indent**: *value* in ems, cm or px, or as a percentage of the window.

**line-height**: *normal* or size, or as a percentage of the font size. Sets the distance between lines of text in a paragraph.

**text-decoration**: *none, underline, overline, line-through* or *blink*.

**text-transform**: *capitalize* (initial), *uppercase, lowercase, none* (used to cancel setting inherited from parent element or style sheet)

# Box properties

These control the size, position and borders of elements.

**width**: size, percentage of window or *auto*.

**height**: size, percentage of window or *auto*.

**float**: *left, right* or *none*.

**clear**: *none, left, right* or *both*.

**margin-top**, **margin-right**, **margin-bottom**, **margin-left**: size, percentage of window or *auto*.

**margin**: scts all margins at once. If one size is given, it is applied to all sides. If four are given, they are read as top, right, bottom and left. If there are two or three, the missing values are taken from the opposite side.

**padding-top**, **padding-right**, **padding-bottom**, **padding-left**: size, or percentage of window.

**padding:** sets all four at once, as **margin**.

**border-top-width**, **border-right-width**, **border-bottom-width**, **border-left-width**: *thin, medium, thick* or size.

**border-width:** sets all border widths at once. As margin except that if two sizes are given, top and bottom widths are set to the first, right and left are set to the second.

**border-color**: from one to four colour names or values, applied to the sides as for **border-width**.

**border-style**:  one to four of *none, dotted, dashed, solid, double, groove, ridge, inset, outset*, applied to the sides as for **border-width** above.

**border**: up to three values to set border-width, border-style and color for all four sides at once.

# Lists

**list-style-type**: *disc, circle, square, decimal, lower-roman, upper-roman, lower-alpha, upper-alpha* or *none*.
Combines the Ul and OL TYPE options for the <LI> tag.

**list-style-image**: *url(hyperlink or filename)* or *none*.
Sets an image as the bullet for a list item.

**list-style-position**: *inside* or *outside*.
Sets the position of the bullet in relation to the list item.

# Miscellaneous

**display**: *block, inline, list-item or none* (turns off the display of the element). Elements fall naturally into three categories: block, e.g. P, H1 and IMG; inline, e.g. B and I; and list-item, LI. They can be redefined into another category – though you would need a convincing reason to mess with this!

**white-space**: *normal, pre* (as <PRE> tag) or *nowrap*.

**A:link**, **A:visited**, **A:active** colour_value.
These are 'pseudo-classes' used to set alternative colours for the anchor tag.

## Take note

The Cascading Style Sheet specification contains some additional options which have been omitted here as they have not yet been implemented in either of the major browsers. You can find the full Level 1 specification at:

http://www.w3.org/TR/REC-CSS1-961217.html

# Links

http://www.jasc.com
> Jasc, for Paint Shop Pro

http://msdn.microsoft.com/developer/
> The Microsoft Developer Network Web site

http://www.hotwired.com/webmonkey/
> Webmonkey, great source of information.

http://www.clicked.com/shareware/
> One of the best shareware stores.

http://www.shareware.com
> Another great shareware center.

http://www.utoronto.ca/webdocs/HTMLdocs/pc_tools.html
> Excellent resource for HTML writers.

http://www.servtech.com/~dougg/graphics/index.html
> Lots of information on the GIF and JPEG formats.

http://www.real.com/products/index.html
> RealNetworks, for RealAudio software.

http://hoohoo.ncsa.uiuc.edu/cgi/
> All about CGI programming

http://www.worldwidemart.com/scripts/
> Matt Wright's site, source of excellent CGI scripts.

http://www.javasoft.com
> Javasoft – get the Java Development Kit from here.

http://www.javasoft.com
> The Java Boutique, a great source of ready-made applets.

http://www.ipswitch.com
> Home of WS_FTP file transfer software.

http://www.w3.org/TR/REC-html40/
> The full HTML 4.0 specification at the World Wide Web Consortium.

# Index

## Symbols

.HTM and .HTML extensions  4
.wav  142
<A HREF = >  38
<A HREF…>  7
<ADDRESS>  26
<APPLET…>  164
<AREA…>  66
<BASE ...>  43
<BASE TARGET=>  95
<BASEFONT SIZE = >  28
<BGSOUND…>  140
<BLOCKQUOTE>  26
<BODY>  6, 30
<BR>  20
<BUTTON…>  132
<CAPTION>  74
<CENTER>  23
<COL…>  84
<COLGROUP…>  84
<DD>  34
<DIV>  115
<DL>  34
<DT>  34
<EMBED …>  140
<FIELDSET>  134
<FONT COLOR = >  30
<FONT FACE =>  32
   in tables  79
<FONT SIZE = >  28
<FORM>  124
<FRAME…>  92
<FRAMESET…>  92
<H…>  21
<HEAD>  6
<HR>  21
<HTML>  6

<IMG SRC…>  60
<INPUT…>  126
<LABEL>  135
<LEGEND>  134
<LI>  34
<LINK>  120
<MAP…>  66
<MARQUEE…>  149
<META …>  6, 172
<NOFRAMES>  180
<NOSCRIPT>  187
<OL>  34
<OPTION>  130
<P>  20
<PARAM>  166
<PRE>  27
<SCRIPT>  153
<SELECT>  130
<SPAN>  115
<STYLE>  101
<TABLE…>  74
<TBODY…>  82
<TD>  74
<TEXTAREA…>  126
<TFOOT…>  82
<THEAD…>  82
<TITLE>  6
<TR>  74
<UL>  34

## A

Address  26
Alignment  23
   images  60
Anchors  40
Angle brackets  4
Animations  146

## B

Background images  58
Backgrounds
  in style sheets  108
Block elements  110
BODY colours  30
BORDER
  frames  97
  images  64
  tables  86
BORDERCOLOR, frames  97
Borders, in style sheets  110
Buttons
  customised  133
  in forms  132

## C

CELLPADDING  76
Cells in tables
  alignment options  78
  merging  90
  size  80
CELLSPACING  76
Checkboxes, forms  128
Classes, style sheets  112
Colour  29
  in style sheets  108
COLSPAN  90
Columns, groups in tables  84
Composer  12
  publishing from  176
Compression  57
Contact details  26
Coordinates  66
CSS1  100

## D

defaultStatus  157

Definition list  34
Document structure  4
Domain  38

## E

Element  102
em  106
Event handlers  155
Excite, registering your site  173

## F

Feedback  124, 159
Feedback forms  46
Fieldsets, in forms  134
File Transfer Protocol  17
file://  47
Files, organising  170
Flash  148
Float, style sheets  117
Folders  171
Font colour  30
Font size  28
Font styles  25
Fonts, in style sheets  104
Forward slash  4
Frame, formatting  97
Frames  92
FrontPage  10
  and image maps  68
FrontPage Express  10
FTP (File Transfer Protocol)  174
ftp://  47
Functions  153

## G

GIF animator  17
GIF graphics format  55
  animated  146

gopher:// 47
Graphics formats 50
Graphics Library 52
Graphics software 14

## H

Hand-coding 13
Headings 21
Hexadecimal numbers (for colours) 29
Hotspot 66
HREF 38
HTML documents 4
HTML editors 10
HTML versions 2
http: (HyperTexT Protocol) 38
Hypertext links 38

## I

IDs, style sheets 112
Images
  alignment 60
  Background 58
  BORDER 64
  creating 52
  in pages 60
  positioning 60
  size 62
  tiled 58
Image Composer 16
Image maps 66
Inheritance 102
Inline style definitions 114
Internet Explorer 4.0 2

## J

JPEG graphics format 57

## L

Labels, in forms 135

Layers, style sheets 117
Layout
  in style sheets 117
  of code 4
Layout methods 72
Line break 20
Link types 47
Links 7, 38
  and targets 95
Lists 34
Lycos, registering your site 173

## M

Macromedia 148
Mailto: 46
Map Edit 69
Margins, style sheets 110
Marquees 149
Media Player 145
Menus, in forms 130
Microsoft Web publishing wizard 177, 178
MIDI 142
mp3 142
Multi-page structures 42

## N

Netscape Composer 12
Netscape Navigator 4.0 2
news: 47
Notepad, for writing HTML 8

## O

onClick 155
onFocus 155
onMouseOver 155
Ordered (numbered) list 34

## P

Padding 110
Paint Shop Pro 14, 53
Paragraph 20
Parent and child 103
Passwords, forms 127
Paths to files 43, 171
Phrasal elements 25
Pre-formatted text 27

## Q

Quotations 26

## R

Radio buttons, forms 128
RealAudio 144
RealNetworks 144
Reset button 132
RGB colours 29
ROWSPAN 90
RULES, in tables 86

## S

Search engines 173
SGML 2
Shockwave 148
Size, images 62
Size of text 28
Sound files 140
Sound Recorder 142
Space 7
Standard Generalized Markup Language 2
Status line 157
Structure tags 6
Style sheets 100
    backgrounds 108
    borders 110
    colours 108
    fonts 104
    margins 110
    text formatting 106
Submit button 132

## T

Tables 74
    formatting 76
    IE 4.0 extensions 82
    planning 88
Targets for links 95
TEXT COLOR 79
Text formatting 20, 25
    in style sheets 106
Text inputs, forms 126
Text layout 6
Typefaces 32

## U

Unordered (bulleted) list 34
Uploading 175
URL 38
URL (Uniform Resource Locator) 38
USEMAP 66

## V

Video clips 145

## W

Web space, accessing 174
white space 7
WIDTH, of cells in tables 80
Windows Media 144
WordPad, for writing HTML 8
WS_FTP 17, 174

## Y

Yahoo, registering your site 173